Streetwise

Street names in and around Birmingham

by
Vivian Bird

Meridian Books

Published 1991 by Meridian Books

© Vivian Bird 1991

British Library Cataloguing in Publication Data

Bird, Vivian

Streetwise: Street names in and around Birmingham

   1. West Midlands 2. Road names

   I. Title

   914.2496

   ISBN 1-869922-11-5

Meridian Books
40 Hadzor Road
Oldbury
Warley
West Midlands
B68 9LA

Printed in Great Britain by BPCC Wheatons Ltd., Exeter.

Introduction

Names fascinate me — forenames, surnames, placenames, pub names, and especially house names which I am always collecting. Names almost always have their story and have contributed much to my writing over many years.

So I was delighted when asked to do a *Streetwise* series in the *Evening Mail*, incorporating the origin of the names of streets with any touch of history associated with them. The series aroused considerable interest. Many readers wrote saying they were making scrapbooks of the *Streetwise* pieces; others asking if they were to appear in book form.

Here, then, they are, with thanks to the editor of the *Evening Mail* for permission to publish in book form those that appeared in his columns — and with many more previously unpublished.

You may not find your own street in this book — Birmingham has so many of them. You will, however, find streets that you know. The occasional intruders — from Redditch, Tamworth, West Bromwich, etc. — spring from the Editor's dictum to "remember our circulation area stretches far beyond Birmingham".

My thanks for help with the occasional name go to Bob Marsden, the Small Heath historian; Mr J.F.Turner of the Engineer's Department of Birmingham City Council who, along with builders, developers and city councillors, has much to do with the choice of street names; and to Victor Skipp, some of whose erudite writings have pointed me in the right direction.

Birmingham lacks any outstanding street names comparable with The Land of Green Ginger (Hull); Whipmawhopmagate (York); or There and Back Again (Bristol). The city does, however, have many street names which throw interesting light on its history, particularly through great families in land-owning, politics, industry and social affairs. You will know Birmingham better when you have read this book.

Vivian Bird, March 1991

Dedication

In dedicating this book to
CAMP HILL RUGBY FOOTBALL CLUB
I am thanking the club for happy
seasons as a spectator and, long ago,
as a modest player with
Camp Hill Old Edwardians.

CAMP HILL is the street name most closely associated with my life in Birmingham. My earliest visits to the city, during the First World War, were to stay with my Harris cousins at the confectioners shop of S.T.Harris, 68 Camp Hill, three doors from the famous Ship Inn. Then, resident in Birmingham, I attended Camp Hill Grammar School from 1921 to 1926, and have always retained close links with the school.

Also by the author:

Bird's Eye View — The Midlands (Roundwood Press, 1969)
The Sunset Coasts (Roundwood Press, 1970)
Portrait of Birmingham (Robert Hale, 1970)
Warwickshire (Batsford, 1973)
Staffordshire (Batsford, 1974)
Short History of Warwickshire (Batsford, 1977)
Exploring the West Midlands (Batsford, 1977)
The Shakespeare Country and the Cotswolds (Ward Lock, 1982)
By Lock and Pound (M and M Baldwin, 1988)

In preparation: The Priestley Riots, July 1791 (Midland Institute)

About the Author

Vivian Bird was born at Warwick on Hallowe'en Day, 1910. He came to Birmingham in 1917 and, living in Sparkbrook, was educated at King Edward VI Grammar School, Camp Hill, and later at Alsager College, Cheshire where he took

a Teachers Emergency Training Course. He was married in 1937 and has one son and twin daughters.

He worked in politics, served in the Royal Artillery from 1940 to 1945, and then taught at Oldknow School, Small Heath until 1951 when he joined the *Birmingham Weekly Post* as a feature writer. In 1960 he became a feature writer for the *Sunday Mercury*, a post he held until his retirement in 1975.

Since retirement he writes as much as ever, including book reviews and essays for the *Birmingham Post* and articles for county magazines. He is much in demand as a public speaker, particularly on journalism and *Streetwise*. He has written nine books, in addition to this volume and a book on the Priestley Riots which is due to be published later this year.

He is a past President of the Midland Area of the Ramblers' Association and pioneered the now nationally famous Six Shropshire Summits Walk.

He has a passion for Ireland which he has visited seventy-five times, having stayed in all thirty-two counties. He also loves gardening, rugger, cruising and classical music. He hates pop, rock and motor-cars!

Vivian Bird was awarded an O.B.E. in the New Years Honours List in 1984.

The main items in this book are arranged in alphabetical order. However, in addition to the main entries there are references to many other streets which you will find listed in the 'Streets' index commencing on page 89. A general index will be found on page 92.

A B ROW   Aston

Until 1911 this thoroughfare was the boundary between the Borough of Aston Manor and Birmingham, but, by the Greater Birmingham Act of that year, Birmingham swallowed up Kings Norton, Yardley, Northfield, Erdington, Handsworth and Aston Manor. Previously Aston Manor had its own representative at

Westminster, one of the most colourful being George Kynoch. Around 1850 this young Scot

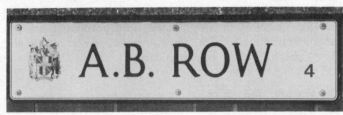

came to Birmingham as a bank clerk, but moved to a Whittall Street factory making percussion caps and was soon manager, and of a powder magazine and factory at Witton. This latter he acquired, and as Kynoch and Company it prospered on cartridge contracts for the War Office. George entered Parliament as Conservative MP for Aston Manor, but when his financial affairs got into disarray he did a 'Stonehouse'. Without resigning his seat, he decamped without his wife in 1888 to the Transvaal, and remained there until his death in 1891 leaving his constituents unrepresented during those three years.

ABERDEEN STREET   Winson Green

One trick in seeking the origin of a street name is to see if it forms a theme with neighbouring streets. Aberdeen Street's neighbours, Carlisle Street and Peel Street, are also place names but are unrelated to Aberdeen. There is also Lansdowne Street and the four add up to statesmen connected with the government of Lord Aberdeen (1852-55). It was a coalition of Aberdeen's Liberals and Tory 'Peelites' who followed the late Sir Robert Peel in opposing the Corn Laws against more aristocratic Tories. The Seventh Earl of Carlisle was Lord Lieut. of Ireland (1853-58), and the Forth Marquess of Lansdowne, Under Secretary of the Foreign Office (1856-58). So Aberdeen Street is named after the Prime Minister who declared war (the Crimean War) against Russia in 1854.

ADA ROAD   Small Heath

Can any reader tell me who Ada, Mona, Emmeline and Robert were, who gave their names to streets approaching St Andrew's (to which Birmingham Football Club came in 1906 from the 'Celery Trenches', Muntz Street)? Ada Road Schools housed a thriving Adult Bible Class in the 1920s, its cricket team noted for fast bowler, Vic Amiss, father of Dennis. Ada Road ABC was founded in 1880 by

Charles Richards who owned the Beehive Warehouse, Albert Street, and the original Rackhams; while Lewis S Richards established 'The House That Jack Built', Newtown Row. They both came from Wales as poor boys. Lewis left £600,000.

ALBANY ROAD Harborne

From its proximity to Regent and Clarence Roads, this is obviously another 'royal' road.The name Albany came from Albany city and county in New York State, a Dutch possession which became English. Charles I was Duke of York and Albany, as were the second sons of George II and George III. With Leopold Charles Edward, Queen Victoria's grandson, the Dukedom of Albany, inherited at his posthumous birth, went to Germany where the Duke later became also Duke of Saxe-Coburg-Gotha. Supporting Germany in World War I, he was struck of the roll of Knights of the Garter.

ALEXANDRA ROAD Edgbaston

Street names often date a property development. Alexandra Road and Princess Road of terraced houses off Belgrave Road commemorate the Danish princess whom Edward VII, as Prince of Wales, married in 1863. From 1854 to 1856 Britain had fought the Crimean War, and with their French and Sardinian allies had used the Bulgarian Black Sea port of Varna. So along with the Princess development went Varna Road, now hidden as Belgravia Close — for Varna Road was Birmingham's notorious red light district between the wars. In 1970 a Garda Siochana officer in Mayo, having enquired into my bonafides and discovered that I came from Birmingham said 'Then you'll be knowing Varna Road'.

'Yes', I replied, 'though not in the nature of business. When were you there?'

'Sure, sorr', he said, 'I've never left Ireland, but all my friends returning from Birmingham tell me about Varna Road'.

ALMA STREET Aston

The Alma River in the Crimea, an Allied victory, is perpetuated in a girl's name (remember actress Alma Taylor who starred with Henry Edwards and Owen Nares in the 1920s?) and fifteen street names in the Birmingham A to Z. Alma Street, Aston was the birthplace of the musician Albert W Ketelby, born at No. 41 on 9 August 1875. At 22 he was musical director of the Vaudeville Theatre, London. His songs enjoyed great popularity earlier this century — *In a Monastery Garden, In a Persian Market, Bells Across the Meadow, The Sanctuary of the Heart*, etc. Ketelby died at Cowes, Isle of Wight, 26 November 1959.

ALSTON STREET Ladywood

Charles Alston Smith-Ryland (*see* Ryland Street) lived at Barford Hill, Sherbourne, near Warwick, owning considerable land thereabouts, features of which reappear as street names not far from Alston Street in the Ladywood territory of the Smith-Rylands — Coplow Hill, Marroway Turn, Morville,

Northbrook Farm, Barford Hill and Sherbourne itself. The family also owns much of Sparkhill. Off Showell Green Lane, roads are named after Charles's daughters Esme, Adria and Doris, and after his son Ivor Phipson. Evelyn Road, off Stratford Road, is another daughter, and Dennis Road, off Taunton Road, another son; while Eton Road reminds us that the wealthy Smith-Ryland boys were Etonians. Sir Charles Smith-Ryland, Charles Alston's grandson, Lord Lieutenant of Warwickshire, died in 1989. There is an Alston Road off Bordesley Green.

ANDOVER STREET   Off Fazeley Street

Near Birmingham Proof House. Named after Mary, Viscountess Andover, of Elford Hall, Staffordshire, who, in 1807 married William, Viscount Andover, oldest son of the Earl of Suffolk and Berkshire. Mary was the daughter of Heneage Finch, second Earl of Aylesford. He brought the Aylesford earls to Packington, Meriden, by marrying Mary Fisher, heiress to the estate. Viscountess Andover was also the descendant of Charles Jennens (*see* Jennens Road), the wealthy owner of much of Duddeston and the Curzon Street area. She became an administrator and beneficiary of the fortune of Charles Jennens's millionaire ancestor William Jennens.

ARMOURY ROAD   Small Heath

Saw the birth of the Birmingham Small Arms Company (BSA) in 1863, an association of fourteen Birmingham gunsmiths first formed in 1854 to supply guns for the Crimean War. They built the Armoury Road factory on condition that the Great Western Railway provided a station nearby — 'Small Heath and Sparkbrook'. A boom during the Franco-Prussian War was followed by a slump, with skilled gunsmiths preparing ponds and flower beds in Small Heath Park. In 1880 E C F Otto rode his newly-invented bicycle on the board room table, and BSA began making bicycles. A record 2,500 rifles were made in a week during the Boer War ; 10,000 Lee-Enfield rifles a week during the Kaiser's War. A motor cycle at £50, and then car-making came before 1914. During an air raid on 14 November 1940 fifty-three employees were killed and eighty-nine injured. Two nights later the entire factory was evacuated.

ARNOLD ROAD   Shirley

Arnold and Ralph Roads, and Arnold Grove, Shirley, are named after two brothers Silverstone, both now deceased, of an estate agent's firm of that name in Birmingham. Arnold, born in 1911 and educated at Llanelli and Swansea University College, was an active Conservative, one time party treasurer and an unsuccessful parliamentary candidate in East Ham. He was knighted in 1964, and in 1974 was created a life peer as Baron Ashdown. Verstone Road, off Ralph Road, comes from a modest beheading of the family name Silverstone. Arnold was once Master of the Worshipful Company of Needlemakers, and a Freeman of the City of London.

ASBURY ROAD   Wednesbury

Named after Francis Asbury (1745–1816), known as 'The Prophet of the Long
Road' Sent to America by John Wesley in 1771 he became first bishop of the

American Methodist
Church. During forty-
five years ministry in
America he travelled
nearly 300,000 miles
on horseback and sent
out circuit mission-
aries in the back-
woods. Wesley was
disgusted   when
Asbury allowed him-
self to be called
bishop. His youthful
home, Asbury Cot-
tage, Newton Road,
West Bromwich, was
dedicated as his perpe-
tual memorial by the
World   Methodist
Council after a 1959
restoration. Asbury

*Bishop Asbury's Cottage, now open to the public and one of
Sandwell's major tourist attractions.*

has an equestrian statue in Washington, DC.

AUBREY ROAD   Small Heath

Although Aubrey Road was my first Birmingham home, and I came to know it
as surrounded by names appertaining to the Digby family (*see* Dora Road), Aubrey
completely eluded me. Then, one day, I saw in Barford Church, Warwickshire, a
memorial to Aubrey John, Lord Somerville, died 28 August 1870, aged 32. I knew
the Somervilles to be noble, as Mary Somerville, married to the Revd Charles
Digby in 1775, was the daughter of the Hon. Hugh Somerville — hence Hugh and
Somerville Roads, Small Heath. So here, surely, was my Aubrey, whose dates
coincided with the development of the Digby Small Heath territory.

AUCKLAND ROAD   Sparkbrook

I am uncertain about this and vaguely remember hearing the name related to
someone emigrating to New Zealand. But it is next off Stratford Road after
Priestley and Erasmus Roads, and one of Priestley's friends and supporters was
William Eden, who in 1793 became Baron Auckland, County Durham. He held a
number of ambassadorial and government posts, and it was to him that Priestley
wrote on 25 March 1794 to obtain a letter of protection for his party — against

Algerian pirates — while sailing to American exile aboard the *Sansom*, a protection readily granted.

BAGNALL LANE West Bromwich

At the end of the eighteenth century John Bagnall, a Tipton ground bailiff, bought mines at Toll End, Coppice and Lea Bank. He then bought a furnace and established an iron business as John Bagnall and Sons. He built Golds Green Furnaces, and purchased Toll End Ironworks which name you will see on many of the bridges on the Birmingham Canal, and Lea Brook Ironworks.

One of the bridges from the Toll End works on the Birmingham Canal.

A Bagnall girl married a Thomas Davis of Golds Hill, and a corn milling business of Davis and Bagnall operated from Golds Hill Mill into the late nineteenth century. It is usual to call cul-de-sacs 'Pudding Bags', but one such, now gone, off Bagnall Lane bore the actual name Pudding Bag Street.

BAKER STREET Small Heath

Off Muntz Street. Named after Councillor George Baker who became Mayor of Birmingham when Joseph Chamberlain, the existing mayor, was elected in a by-election to the House of Commons on 27 June 1875. Baker had a second term in 1876–77. A wealthy Quaker businessman, Baker had a mansion, Boscastle, off the Ludlow Road outside Bewdley. He gave Ruskin some twenty acres, called St George's Land, near Bewdley, on which to set up a crafts centre. Hawkes Street commemorates an earlier Mayor Of Birmingham, Henry

Hawkes (1852–53), and also off Muntz Street, Wright Street recalls John Skirrow Wright (b. 1822), social reformer and industrialist, whose statue once stood in Victoria Square, later in Chamberlain Place, now in the Council House entrance hall. Wright died at a meeting in the Council House in 1880.

BALSALL HEATH ROAD   Balsall Heath

To reduce a two mile journey to three quarters of a mile, this road came into being from an agreement in August 1829 between the owners of the Edgbaston Estate and the Long Moors and Balsall Heath Estate. It aimed 'to form at a cost of at least £1,000 a direct line of road 36 ft. wide from Worcester Road (now Bristol Road) opposite Wellington Road, across Pershore Road and the River Rea to the Alcester Road near Mr Haden's residence'. There is an old Haden Street off Alcester Road, and the new Haden Way now cuts across Balsall Heath Road.

BARCLAY ROAD   Warley

Named after Lucy Barclay of the banking family, preposterously said to be the daughter of George III and Hannah Lightfoot, known as 'the Fair Quakeress'. Lucy was married to gun-maker Samuel Galton junior (Galton Road is parallel with Barclay Road) who purchased the Warley Estate for £7,300. The Estate was inherited by one of his sons, Hubert, who built a Gothic mansion there, Warley Abbey — demolished by Birmingham Corporation in 1957 — famed for the ghost of a grey lady, sketched and reproduced by Harry Furniss, the Punch artist. This branch of the Galtons moved to Hadzor House, near Droitwich, in 1821 — so Hadzor Road in the Warley area.

BARGEHORSE WALK   Hawkesley

This road is practically above the Wast Hill Tunnel on the Worcester and Birmingham Canal, and is part of the route across the Wast Hills on which horses were led while the narrow-boats they hauled were taken through the 2,726 yds tunnel by tug — or maybe legged through. The canal was begun at the Birmingham end in 1795 and completed to Worcester in 1815. Many middle-aged Brummies will remember cruises from Lifford to Tardebigge in the 1950s on *Norman Chamberlain*, the Birmingham Boys' Clubs' narrow-boat, of which I, as honorary skipper, made several passages of the Wast Hill Tunnel — a journey of some thirty minutes. On bright days the far portal of the tunnel could be seen as a pin-point of light from either end.

BASKERVILLE ROAD   off Broad Street

This road, with Baskerville House (Council offices), recalls a macabre story. John Baskerville, born Wolverley, Worcestershire in 1706 and famed as a type-founder, held various offices in Birmingham. As an atheist, dying in 1775, he was buried in his garden at Easy Hill (Easy Row). His coffin was dug up during canal construction in 1821 and lay in a warehouse until 1829, opened occasionally and the corpse inspected and described. In 1829 the coffin was moved to Job Marston's shop in Monmouth Street (Colmore Row), thence clandestinely into Vault 521 (Mr Knott's) in Christ Church catacombs, Victoria Square. There it was opened in 1893 before an invited audience, closed again, remaining there for five years until the demolition of Christ Church, when Baskerville went to his present resting place in Warstone Lane Cemetery on 26 February 1898. Pieces of Baskerville's shroud turn up occasionally — I once saw one attached to an ancient book.

BEACON ROAD   Great Barr

Obviously Barr Beacon, which was purchased in 1918 by Colonel J H Wilkinson of Ashfurlong Hall, Sutton Coldfield, and presented to the public as a memo-

rial to men of the Warwickshire and Staffordshire regiments who fell in the Kaiser's War. The dome on the beacon was erected in 1933 in memory of Col. Wilkinson. During the Hitler War, in common with all aids to direction, the toposcope was removed from Barr Beacon — to the museum at Cannon Hill Park where it was destroyed by a bomb. A flaming beacon is the crest of the Scott baronets of Great Barr.

BELLS LANE

Druids Heath

From Bell's Farm. Before the present road was constructed the lane from Maypole to Kings Norton passed through the farmyard.

The memorial dome on Barr Beacon.

Over 700 years ago Henry III gave William de Belne the nearby property of Blackgrave. Under the name of Bell the family lived at Northfield where they gave their name to Bell Holloway — 'holloways' were early roads, so called because traffic on them wore hollow trenches. The Bell Inn, Northfield probably takes its name from the family. There is still a Blackgrave Farm three miles south of Druids Heath where a ghostly carriage and four is said to disappear into a pond.

BERRY HALL LANE   Solihull

From Berry Hall nearby, built by Joseph Gillott II, son of Joseph Gillott (*see* Gillott Road). Joseph II inherited the pen business on the death of his father at

Stanmore, Middlesex — hence Stanmore Road in Gillott's Rotton Park territory. Joseph I left his property to his twelve grand-children, one of them, Algernon Sydney, being remembered in Algernon Road, Edgbaston. Algernon's son, Bernard, became the last Gillott to have his own road — Bernard Road off City Road. Berry Hall was built around 1870, and its gates feature on engravings of the pens which brought fortune to the Gillotts. These gates have been removed to Wiltshire.

BETHOLOM ROW near Five Ways

Beth Olom — City of the Dead. A narrow passage off Islington Row near Five Ways, no longer in the A to Z but recently retaining vestiges of its nameplate. It borders an old Jewish burial ground, acquired in 1823 and used for burials until the 1870s. The Jews, centred in this area, were unlucky that their cemeteries were close to Birmingham's developing railways. The Froggery itself disappeared and its cemetery sold for £260 in 1849 when New Street station was built. Granville Street Cemetery went with Birmingham West Suburban Railway (Harborne line), and Beth Olom was threatened by the Midland Railway, but the House of Commons supported a deviation suggested by Birmingham's Jewish community.

BIRCHALL STREET Deritend

Named after a grove of birch trees long since gone. Off it is the Stone Yard, to which in the 1880s came Walter Frederick Bannocks, newly-established as a mason in marble, granite and slate. His successors, W F Bannocks (Senr.) Ltd. of Hall Green, have put a polished sheen of marble 'cladding' on many of Birmingham's buildings since the Second World War.

BISHOP STREET Lower Edgbaston

Sir Thomas Gooch of a Suffolk family was Bishop of Ely and married three times. His first wife was Mary Sherlock, daughter of a Dean of St Paul's and sister of Thomas Sherlock, Bishop of London. To supplement his episcopal stipend, in 1730 Bishop Sherlock purchased for speculation a tract of Birmingham from the Marrow family. This was eventually inherited by the bishop's nephew, Sir Thomas, the third Gooch baronet, who began to develop this area. He showed his gratitude by naming two adjacent streets off Gooch Street, Bishop Street and Sherlock Street. The Gooch seat in Suffolk is Benacre Hall, Wrentham, hence Benacre and Wrentham streets in the Gooch territory; while Hope Street and Vere Street compliment Harriet Hope Vere, wife of Sir Edward Sherlock Gooch, the seventh baronet.

BISSELL CLOSE Hall Green

Off Gresham Road, commemorates John Bissell, whose will in 1727 gave an annuity and rent-charge to pay the schoolmaster of Hall Green 40 shillings each Michaelmas Day, and 20 shillings to buy a coat for one poor man in the

Swanshurst Quarter of Yardley Parish, to be marked J B on the left sleeve. These payments became a rent-charge on James Taylor (Taylor Road, Kings Heath) of Whorstock Farm (Warstock Lane). Humphrey Greswolde (Greswolde Road, Sparkhill and elsewhere) in 1671 left a £5 annuity to provide four gowns of blue cloth, with H G in red cloth, for four poor men, one from each quarter of Yardley Parish.

BLAKE LANE   Bordesley Green

From 'Bleak' the highest point of Small Heath at 735 ft. Famed for The Custard House pub, its name a mystery though obviously from being on the site of Custard House Farm. Bob Marsden, Small Heath's leading historian, thinks the 'costard', a large round apple, was grown in the farm orchards. In 1853 William Woodstock purchased The Little Croft on the farm, built The Custard House, and was licensee until succeeded by his wife. In 1888 the pub was bought by Atkinson's Brewery, Aston.

The quaintly named Custard House pub in Blake Lane probably recalls a nearby orchard where 'costard' apples were grown.

BOOTHS FARM ROAD   Great Barr

In 1808 William Booth was acquitted of murdering his brother John at Hall End Farm, near Henley-in-Arden. Four years later, however, he was hanged — for forgery, also a capital crime. His farm at Great Barr was found to be the headquarters of a thriving forging industry. William went to the gallows at Stafford, the lever was pulled, the trap opened, Booth disappeared — but so did the rope which had not been secured! Recovering from his 12 ft. drop, Booth was returned to the scaffold, but this time the mechanism failed; and three times the unfortunate forger had to signal the 'ready' before he was successfully hanged.

BORDESLEY HIGH STREET   Bordesley

Bordesley Palace Theatre, forever associated with Ruby Kimberley (a leading actress and pantomime principal boy), is gone. Clyde Street, alongside the theatre where one queued, survives. Opposite the theatre was the café and sweet shop kept by boxer Joe Fox, who displayed his Lonsdale Belt in the window. Warner Street, also surviving, had the charming Dowell's Retreat, almshouses for old ladies, now in Moseley. Early last century Aston Borough Gaol was in High Street, attached to the Brown Lion pub. In 1830 Jemima Brownell kept the pub and W D Brownell kept the gaol, known as Brownell's Hole.

BOURNVILLE LANE   Bournville

Bournville — simply the village on the Bourn Brook. Residents enjoying the sylvan peace of George Cadbury's conception that a house should occupy only a quarter of its site, the remainder being garden, as decreed in his 1900 Bournville Village Trust, might not know that a model community which inspired Bournville is now the most war-torn spot in the United Kingdom. George Cadbury had Quaker friends in Northern Ireland, the Richardsons, who had linen mills at Bessbrook in South Armagh. In the mid nineteenth century John Grubb Richardson set up his model village — good housing, no pub, no pawnshop — and no police except the Bessbrook Spinning Company's own 'policeman', Joe Milligan, an athlete armed with a walking stick. Today Bessbrook is a beleaguered garrison.

BOWCROFT GROVE   Pype Hayes

An insignificant grove near Pype Hayes Park which perpetuates a bit of ancient local history. In medieval times a stone cottage near the park, called Bow Bearers' Lodge, housed two bowmen, retainers of the Earl of Warwick, whose job was to escort travellers across Sutton Chase, now Sutton Park but then a wild and desolate tract, the haunt of robbers and other malefactors. The lodge was demolished in 1828 but a field thereabouts was still called Bow Bearers' Croft, and it was on this site that Bowcroft Grove was developed.

BRACEBRIDGE ROAD   Sutton Coldfield

In 1419 Richard, Earl of Warwick, let the Manor House of Sutton to Sir Ralph Bracebridge of Kingsbury in return for the services of seventeen bowmen and nine lances. Sir Ralph then built the dam which contains Bracebridge Pool. Pools were constructed to provide fish for Lent, and Bracebridge's rent for the Manor was £10 per annum or 120 bream — at 20 pence a fish. Sir Ralph's granddaughter, Alice Bracebridge and John Arden of Park Hall, near Sutton, were in love. When Arden's father opposed the match, Alice's father led his retainers in an attack on Park Hall and kidnapped a compliant John until his father consented to the marriage. The couple went to Court where John became Lord of the Bedchamber to Henry VII.

BRACEBRIDGE STREET   Aston

The Bracebridge family of Atherstone Hall were kinsmen of the Holtes of Aston Hall, a relationship Abraham Bracebridge claimed in 1790 when unsuccessfully challenging Sir Robert Lawley as MP for Warwickshire, which included Birmingham. The last of the Bracebridges, Charles Holte Bracebridge, died in 1872, and a memorial inscription in Mancetter Church claims his descent on the female side from Egbert, first King of England; Alfred the Great; the Plantagenet kings; from ancient kings of Scotland and Robert Bruce; and from Earls of Mercia, Warwick, and Northumberland

BRADFORD STREET   Bordesley to City

Bradford Street runs from the market area to Holy Trinity Church, Camp Hill. Nothing to do with the Yorkshire town, but with Henry Bradford, a prominent Quaker living in Old Square, described as a timberman. He had inherited the Warner Estate — Warner Street off Bradford Street. Hanson's 1778 map of Birmingham shows the beginnings of Bradford Street after Henry, in 1767, had offered land free to anyone wishing to establish business there. Those who could not afford a stone building were allowed a wooden shed or single room for up to two shillings a week. One of Birmingham's oldest businesses had premises in Bradford Street; Atkin, Sawmaker, 1760. Through several moves, culminating in Bradford Street, there was an Atkin in the firm until 1949. Cooper and Goode, metals; Ingall, Parsons and Clive, funeral furnishers; and George Mason, wholesale groceries, all had Bradford Street premises. Henry Bradford died in 1774.

BRAITHWAITE ROAD   Sparkbrook

From Stratford Road to 'Farm', the old Lloyd residence. In 1791 the first Samuel Lloyd married Rachel Braithwaite of Kendal — hence Kendal Road, north of Farm. Two of Rachel's brothers, George and Isaac, married the sisters Mary and Anne Lloyd in 1806 and 1808. A son of Samuel and Rachel, George Braithwaite Lloyd, married Mary Dearman, which accounts for Dearman Road, the eastern boundary of Farm. The first Lloyd to come to Birmingham, Charles II, had died in 1698 and been buried in the Quaker cemetery in Bull Lane (Bull Street) but this was disturbed when the Great Western Railway tunnelled into Snow Hill. Charles's skull was dug up and remained in the keeping of George Braithwaite Lloyd for years until it was reinterred in the Friends Meeting House graveyard, Bull Street. Some years later this was disturbed again in the 1950s redevelopment.

BRAY'S ROAD   Sheldon

In 1922 Bishop Hamilton Baines, Rector of Birmingham, was presented with
the State Flag of Maryland, which he then hung in St Philip's Cathedral. This
was in recognition of the work of Dr Thomas Bray, Rector of Sheldon, who in
1696 was assigned to help the infant church of Maryland. To assist in this work
Dr Bray, in 1698, founded the Society for the Propagation of the Christian
Knowledge. In 1700 he came back to England, and with the sympathy of
William and Mary, then on the throne, he founded the Society for the
Propagation of the Gospel to supply missionaries for overseas. Sheldon was
transferred to Birmingham in 1931, and from only 451 inhabitants in 1921 it
has grown enormously with new housing estates of Lyndon Green and Wells
Green.

BROAD STREET   City

Today, with the new Convention Centre, etc, Broad Street has become one of
Birmingham's most important thoroughfares. It nearly had a 'first' in 1860
when an American inventor, aptly named George Francis Train, sought
permission to construct a tramway from New Street to Five Ways along Broad
Street. Permission was granted by the Public Works Committee, with a
suggested extension along Hagley Road to Monument Road, but Train did not
proceed. Birmingham's first tramway was completed in 1873, linking
Monmouth Street (Colmore Row) with Hockley by horse-drawn tram.

BROOMHALL CRESCENT   Hall Green

Road names often come by several removes. A place-name sometimes derives
from a natural feature. A surname may also do so — or from a place-name thus
derived. The name Broomhall was first a thirteenth century farm where broom
grew, and a resident family took the name. In 1420 the last Broomhall died,
dividing his property between three daughters; and when his son-in-law was
outlawed in 1423 the family property as well as the surname disappeared. The
place-name remained and there was still a Broomhall Mill in the late eighteenth
century on the Wesley Brook, its site now incorporated in Fox Hollies Park,
half a mile distant from the moated Broomhall which occupied the present site
of Broomhall Crescent.

BULL STREET   City

In Tudor times it was Chapel Street, from the chapel of St Thomas's Priory. It
took its present name from the Old Bull Tavern with its bowling green. Bull
Street was bisected by Corporation Street around 1880. The pharmaceutical
supplier, Philip Harris, occupied No. 1 and No. 9 before moving to Edmund
Street. No. 3, the Red Lion, was the headquarters of Birmingham's Free
Debating Society in the 1770s. Wrighton's 1818 directory lists Richard Cadbury
at No. 92 as 'linen draper and silk merchant'. Richard's son, John, eventually

had a tea and coffee shop next door, but moved to Crooked Lane to establish a cocoa and chocolate business — which led to Bournville.

BUSHMORE ROAD   Hall Green

On 25 April 1910 at the Grand Hotel, Birmingham, there came up for auction 'Bushmore Farm, Robin Hood, Hall Green, Worcestershire, about 12 acres of pasture having a frontage of about 160 yards on the road from Robin Hood to Solihull, and approached by a private road from Shirley Road together with a cottage of parlour, kitchen, scullery, dairy, pantries, store room and two bedrooms, also three-stall stable with loft; six-tie cowhouse; mixing shed and poultry house; pig stye etc'. The property was then let to Christopher Hodgetts together with a field in Robin Hood Lane at an annual rent of £65.15s. The farmhouse was at the southern end of the present Bushmore Road. The map on the sale marks a race-course over the site of Bushmore Road, with a grandstand alongside Shirley Road.

CALIFORNIA WAY   Bartley Green

Isaac Flavel returned from California, United States, in 1842; bought Stonehouse Farm (Stonehouse Road), and established a brick-making business there. With the profits he built the California Inn, which gave its name to the surrounding district and to the thoroughfare beyond Harborne. Tividale also has a California Road. Could this be an association between digging for gold and quarrying in the adjacent Darby Hills?

CAMP HILL   Bordesley

Incorrectly thought to owe its name to the now-demolished Ship Inn having been Prince Rupert's headquarters in the 1643 Battle of Birmingham. This brought about a corruption of the original name Kempe's Hill — from a farming family with 200 acres thereabouts mentioned as long ago as 1350. King Edward VI Grammar School opened there in 1883, and shops on Camp Hill will be remembered by generations of Camp Hill Old Edwardians — Lazenby's tuck-shop on Ravenhurst Street corner, Harris the confectioner, Coggins the greengrocer, and Baker the newsagent. Camp Hill saw riotous scenes in 1880–83 during controversy over church ritual at Holy Trinity Church.

CANTLOW ROAD   Kings Heath

Surely from Aston Cantlow, Warwickshire, which has the distinction of having the only church in the county which had an incumbent who became a saint. He was St Thomas Cantelupe — of which Cantlow is a corruption. He appears in the east window as Bishop of Hereford which he became in 1275. He later became Chancellor of England. Shakespeare's parents were married in Aston Cantlow church. More recently the village became famous for the duck suppers supplied by the Edkins family at the Kings Head.

CAPE HILL
Smethwick

From The Cape of Good Hope — and in the shadow of Mitchells and Butlers Brewery are two battle names from the South African Wars which we might well wish to forget. Majuba Road commemorates a British disaster at Majuba Hill in February 1881 during the First Boer War, our troops being annihilated and Colley, the commander, killed. Even worse, in the Second Boer War, was Buller's defeat at Colenso, Natal, on the Tugela River, (commemorated in Colenso Road) coming in the 'Black Week' of December 1899, when Generals Methuen and Gatacre were also defeated, respectively at Magersfontein and Stormberg.

CAPERN GROVE
Harborne

Edward Capern, born Tiverton 1819, was a postman based on Bideford, Devon, who composed poetry on his round. In 1868 he came to High Street, Harborne, to be near his son, and became the friend and walking companion of Elihu Burritt of Victoria Road, Harborne, the American Vice-Consul in Birmingham who wrote *Walks in the Black Country and its Green Borderland*. Capern published his *Sungleams and Shadows* in Birmingham with poems on local themes. In 1884 he returned to Devon where he died in 1894 aged 76.

CARDIGAN STREET
Duddeston

An unexpected place to find a memory of the immortal 600 of the Light Brigade who charged the Russian guns at Balaclava in October 1854. Cardigan Street is named after Harriett Georgina Brudenell, second daughter of the 6th Earl of Cardigan, and sister of the seventh Earl who led the Charge of the Light Brigade — and also gave his name to a woollen waistcoat. Harriet's wedded life started auspiciously. Married on 20 March 1820 to Richard William Penn, she became a viscountess on the following day with the death of her husband's paternal grandfather, whose title, Viscount Curzon, Richard inherited along with the Curzon lands around Curzon Street and Duddeston in Birmingham.

CARLESS AVENUE
Harborne

The Carless family is recorded in a burial at Harborne in 1538. They subsequently lived at 'Ravenhurst' (Ravenhust Road). In 1651 one of them, Colonel William Carless, shared Charles II's hiding place in the Boscobel Oak and has a memorial tablet in Brewood Church, Staffordshire. In the eighteenth century one Richard Carless, a lawyer, had a son, the Revd Walter Carless, who married and predeceased a sister of Dr Samuel Johnson's Birmingham friend, the bookseller Edmund Hector. Johnson met her occasionally at Hector's home in Old Square, and he once told Boswell on their way to visit Hector, 'You will see there Mr Hector's sister, Mrs Carless; she was the first woman with whom I was in love'.

CARNAVON ROAD
Bordesley Green

In the current A to Z, off Bordesley Green near Cattell Road–Garrison Lane junction, petering out behind Bordesley Green Secondary School. On the spot, however, there is merely a rough track between Court Steam Laundry and a billiards hall. Bob Marsden, the Small Heath historian, describes it as 'The Road That Never Was'. It is named after Henry Howard Molyneux, 4th Earl of Carnavon, who was Colonial Secretary 1866–67 and 1874–78 — the boss of Charles Bowyer Adderley (later Lord Norton) of Hams Hall, Lea Marston, who was Under-Secretary for the Colonies 1866–68. The Adderleys owned land in Saltley and Bordesley Green area.Edgbaston

CARPENTER ROAD
Edgbaston

Former site of the Midland BBC headquarters, in the Blind School, prior to the move to Pebble Mill. Henry, 1st Lord Calthorpe, married Frances, daughter and co-heir of General Benjamin Carpenter, on 1 May 1783. She died on her forty-fourth wedding anniversary. Their second, third and fourth sons became the 2nd, 3rd and 4th Lords Calthorpe in succession. A fifth son in the Royal Navy was killed in 1816 suppressing a riot in Jamaica, aged 23. Ampton Road, joining Carpenter Road, is named, as is Pakenham Road, Edgbaston, after Suffolk villages in Calthorpe territory. George and Frederick Roads, off Islington Row, are named after the 3rd and 4th Lords Calthorpe.

CARRS LANE
City

Long ago known as Godde's Carte Lane because the cart which carried vessels for communion at St Martin's was kept there. But some have it that God's Cart was a bier for carrying corpses to Park Street burial ground. Others say it was a stage for presenting religious drama. The thoroughfare retained its religious atmosphere with the building by some Congregationalists in 1747 of a meeting house there. This was replaced in the early decades of the last century by Carrs Lane Chapel familiar to many Brummies, more recently replaced by the new Carrs Lane Centre. Carrs Lane Chapel attained national fame from the preaching of the Revd J Angell James, Dr Jowett and Dr Dale.

CARTLAND ROAD
Kings Heath

The Cartland family lived for 100 years at The Priory, Kings Heath until, with the death of Major Howard Cartland in 1940, the governors of King Edward's Grammar School, Camp Hill, negotiated for the purchase of the Priory Estate, and a new school arose there, occupied until 1956. Ronald Cartland was MP for Kings Norton from 1935 until his death in action in 1940. Beside the main path into Tewkesbury Abbey is the Cartland Cross, to Major J B F Cartland of the Worcesters, killed in action 27 May 1918 at Berry-au-Bec, aged 42; and his sons Major Ronald Cartland MP, Worcestershire Yeomanry Anti-Tank Regt.,

The original King Edward VI Grammar School, Camp Hill, with its beautiful first World War memorial gateway. The school moved to Vicarage Road, Kings Heath in 1956 and the old buildings now house the Bordesley Centre.(See Cartland Road)

killed in action near Cassell, aged 33, 30 May 1940, and Captain James Cartland, Lincolnshires, killed in action at Ypres, 29 May 1940, aged 27.

CARVER STREET   Hockley

The Carver family estate bordered the Colmore family estate to the north between the Sandpits and Livery Street. Edward Carver was, in 1789, county steward of the Bean Club, a loyalist meeting place for county gentlemen and town industrialists. He was President of Birmingham Church and King Club, founded in November 1792 — echoing in its title the 'Church and King' slogan of the 1791 Priestley Rioters against the pro-Jacobin Dissenters. When the Militia was increased in 1779 Captain Carver's company of Birmingham Volunteers filled its ranks in five days recruiting at the White Horse, Congreve Street and The Death of General Wolfe in Digbeth.

CASSOWARY ROAD   Handsworth Wood

Arising from the nearby Wesleyan Methodist College for the training of ministers, built in the 1880s and now accommodating students of Aston University. The college arms included a cassowary — an ostrich-like bird — obviously associated with a cynical quotation of Bishop Samuel Wilberforce :

If I were a cassowary
On the plains of Timbuctoo
I would eat a missionary
Cassock, band, and hymn-book too.

Alas, the bishop's ornithology was not up to his sense of humour. The flightless cassowary is indigenous to the East Indies, not Africa.

CHRIST CHURCH STEPS   City

No longer in the A to Z as Christ Church Passage, the steps are still there, rising from New Street to Waterloo Street beside Victoria Square. Christ Church stood on the corner of Waterloo Street and Colmore Row. The foundation stone was laid on 22 July 1805 by the Earl of Dartmouth, substituting for George III who gave £1,000 to the building fund, but was prevented from laying the stone as he hoped by gout. The church was consecrated in 1813. With population declining in the city centre, Christ Church was demolished at the turn of the century, St Agatha's, Sparkbrook, being built in its stead and incorporating Christ Church font, clock and bell. With the demolition of Galloway's Corner, the exposed steps provide a fine elevation for viewing the Council House.

CLARENCE ROAD   Harborne

Alone, any Clarence Road might be someone's forename. With Regent and Albany Roads adjacent it is a dukedom, obviously named after the Duke of Clarence, third son of George III, who became King William IV. Regent refers to the Prince Regent, George III's eldest son and Prince of Wales, who became

George IV. Albany, favoured for hotel names, is an ancient Scottish title of the Dukes of York. This particular Duke of York and Albany was Frederick Augustus, second son of George III. As Commander-in-Chief of His Majesty's Forces he was the 'Grand Old Duke of York' of the song 'who had ten thousand men' and marched them up and down that satirical hill.

CLAY LANE

Yardley

Appropriately enough, bounding Yardley Cemetery and with a pub 'Journey's End' — but it is named after Henry Clay, the Birmingham inventor of papier mâché, examples of such work being displayed at Blakesley Hall Museum, Yardley. Though similar

The Angel Drinking Fountain, originally in the material had been used in *churchyard of Christ Church, now in St Philips'* japanned trays and snuff *churchyard. (See Christ Church Steps)* boxes, Clay, in 1772, patented his process of manufacturing boards of papier mâché, susceptible in use as wood worked by cabinet makers' tools. Clay made a large fortune and was High Sheriff of Warwickshire in 1790 — his profit on a £5 8s 9d tray was £3 8s 2d. He presented Queen Charlotte with a sedan chair made of papier mâché. On the expiry of his patent, papier mâché work became one of Birmingham's major products.

CLAYTON DRIVE

Castle Bromwich

Birmingham was the hub of the English canal system on which the greatest narrow-boat fleet was owned by Fellows, Morton and Clayton. Clayton Drive is named after the Clayton Family, which has a memorial in Castle Bromwich Church to Alderman Thomas Clayton of The Cedars, and Forrester Clayton of the canal carriers. In 1910 FMC pioneered the single-cylinder, two-stroke,

Christ Church which originally stood on the New Street–Colmore Row corner and was demolished at the turn of the century. (See Christ Church Steps)

semi-diesel unit in their boats. At waterways nationalization in 1948 FMC went into voluntary liquidation, and the Waterways Executive bought their fleet of 172 craft. Thomas Clayton of Oldbury, bulk carriers of crude tar from gasworks to Oldbury Tar Distillers, was part of the family.

CLODESHALL ROAD   Saltley

Walter de Clodshale, the Lord of Saltley, founded a chantry at St Martin's in 1330, endowing a priest to perform daily services for the souls of himself and Agnes, his wife; and Richard de Clodshale founded a second chantry for similar services. At Henry VIII's 'reformation' these endowments were dispersed. In 1327 Walter de Clodshale was rated at 15 shillings — being a twentieth part of his movables — as a subsidy for the defence of the Kingdom against the Scots. Walter, Thomas and John de Clodshale junior were in the Assize Rolls as jurors.

## CLOPTON ROAD					Chelmsley Wood

Sir Hugh Clopton spanned the Avon at Stratford with Clopton Bridge in 1480–90. Clopton House, a mile north of Stratford, saw two tragedies on which Shakespeare might have drawn. Young Charlotte Clopton, dying of plague in 1564, was hurriedly buried in Clopton Chapel at Holy Trinity Church. When, some time later, the tomb was opened, she was standing at the doorway, dead — and Shakespeare later brought Juliet to life in her tomb. Margaret Clopton drowned herself for love in a pool in Clopton House grounds — a prototype of the mad Ophelia. Clopton House is thought to have inspired the bedchamber where, in *The Taming of the Shrew*, Christopher Sly awoke richly clothed after falling into a drunken sleep in an ale-house.

## COLDBATH ROAD					King's Heath

When a road is named after a natural feature it's a certainty that the feature came first. Coldbath Road is close neighbour with Coldbath Brook which runs from Moseley Golf Course through Coldbath Pool, beneath Yardley Wood Road, and alongside Moseley Bog to the millpool at Sarehole Mill where it helped turn the mill-wheel before its confluence with the River Cole. Coldbath appears elsewhere as a name for a stream. London had a Coldbath Fields — 'where prisoners were held'.

## COLESHILL STREET					City

This led eastward out of Birmingham towards Coleshill, an established community many centuries ago. The street was the location of various entertainments over the years. Early last century cock-fighting took place openly at the New Cock Pit in Coleshill Street. Entertainments at the Old Rodney pub were so successful that in 1846 Holder's Concert Hall was built. This in time became a variety theatre still remembered by older Brummies as the Gaiety.

## COLLEGE ROAD					Springfield

The College, in Wake Green Road, is now incorporated in Moseley Secondary School. Started in 1838 with thirteen students in the Hockley home of its benefactors, the Mansfields, it opened in 1857 as Spring Hill Theological College for training Baptist Ministers. Moving to Wake Green it spent twenty-nine years there, transferring to Oxford in 1886 as Mansfield College. Thereafter the Wake Green building became the Pine Dell Hydropathic, its swimming bath boarded over as the assembly hall of Moseley Grammar School which took over in 1923. Between hydropathic and grammar school the premises were Moseley Botanical Gardens, where, at a wedding in 1896, confetti was first used in England.

COLMORE ROW

City

The Colmores originated at Tournai in France, and on the dissolution of Birmingham's Priory by Henry VIII in 1536 they purchased priory lands for speculation. A William Colmore was a mercer on High Street–Moor Street corner in Tudor times. His son or his grandson built New Hall, the family seat downhill northward of Colmore Row and reached by an elm avenue along what is now Newhall Street. In 1747 a private Act of Parliament enabled Ann Colmore to develop her estates, and Colmore Row from Newhall Street westward was then named Ann Street, while eastward it was Monmouth Street. Great Charles Street is named after Ann's heir — it was previously Great George Street after one of her brothers-in-law; while Edmund Street commemorates another, the Revd Edmund Colmore.

CONGREVE STREET

City

Butchered, first to build the Council house in the 1870s, when Birmingham lost Allin's Cabinet of Curiosities, an eccentric tailor's shop; and in the 1950s to build the Central Library. Taking its name from being the western limit of the Priory 'conigree' (rabbit warren) Congreve Street had previously been Friday Street, where factors paid their journeymen on Fridays — Friday Bridge still spans the canal. This departed street is still dear to Brummie hearts for two cherished institutions — the White Horse Hotel, and Bosley's Pie Shop. Between the wars Birmingham's tallest building stood on Congreve Street and Edmund Street corner — the Norwich Union offices.

CONYBERE STREET

Highgate

Rabbits (coney) in the barley (bere). The splendid church of St Alban in Conybere Street had a troubled origin in 1865. The Revd James Pollock was the first curate of a mission church there, helped by his brother the Revd Tom, who came for a fortnight and stayed twenty-five years — they are

Memorial cross to the Pollock brothers outside St Alban's Church.

Queens Corner, at the junction of New Street and Corporation Street, remembers Queen Victoria's visit to Birmingham in 1887.

This relief of William Shakespeare is on the shop originally occupied by W H Smith.

worthily commemorated by a cross at St Alban's west front. The Pollock's High Church practices were opposed by a Low Church mob who regularly stoned the brothers, and besieged them in St Alban's from Morning Service to Evensong, and harassed them while up to thirty policemen escorted them home. In 1881 the present church was opened, with St Patrick's, Frank Street — now demolished — in 1896. Father James died in 1895, brother Tom a year later.

St Alban's Church, Conybere Street.

CORPORATION STREET City

Driven through a warren of slums between 1878 and 1882 at a cost of around £34,000, this was part of Joseph Chamberlain's 'Improvement Scheme' involving ninety-three acres, the Corporation acquiring the freehold of some forty-five of them, costing £1,300,000. Sites were let to builders on a 75-year lease. Chamberlain said 'This will make Birmingham the richest borough in the Kingdom sixty or seventy years hence'. The properties increased in value over a hundredfold by the time a Conservative Council sold the freeholds in the 1960s. High up on the old Post and Mail building as it turns from New Street into Corporation Street look for the legend 'Queen's Corner' — celebrating Queen Victoria's 1887 visit to open the new Law Courts. Then, several shops up Corporation Street, lower your glance and above the windows of what was once W H Smith's you will see reliefs of Shakespeare and Sir Walter Scott.

CREGOE STREET Lee Bank

Part of Colmore's Bell Barn Estate and named after Frind Cregoe, on whom Caroline Colmore, dying in 1837, settled her estate on the understanding that he added Colmore to his name. Back in the city centre, Cornwall Street perpetuates Frind's county of origin; Margaret Street his grand-daughter Mrs Margaret Radcliffe; and Barwick (pronounced *Barrick*) Street, behind the Grand Hotel, his grandson William Barwick Cregoe-Colmore. Caroline Colmore, her brother Lionel, and sister Mary Ann all have streets named after them in the Jewellery Quarter. They were the children of Charles Colmore — the Great Charles Street man — who died in 1794, and is buried at Hendon, Middlesex. In 1889 the Colmore Estate gave a quarter of an acre for the School of Art, bounded by Cornwall Street and Margaret Street.

CURZON STREET City

(*See also Andover Street, Cardigan Street and Kedleston Road.*)
From a temporary terminus at Vauxhall the first ever train left Birmingham for Liverpool on 4 July 1837. A few hours later the first train arrived from Liverpool. In the following year the line had been extended to Birmingham's first permanent station at Curzon Street. Also in 1838 the London

Plaque on Curzon Street station.

Curzon Street, Birmingham's first main line railway station.

to Birmingham Railway ran into Curzon Street, followed in 1840 by the Birmingham to Gloucester Railway from its previous terminus at Camp Hill Station. Curzon Street Station shared the same architect with Euston Station — Philip Hardwick, who gave Curzon Street facade its four Ionic columns, described by Pevsner in his *Warwickshire (Buildings of England)* as 'an austerely elegant design which must be preserved at all costs'.

DALE END

City

In Westley's 1731 map Dale End was named as Broad Street, and the Welsh Cross stood at the junction of Bull, or Chapel, Street with Broad Street. By 1784 the name of Dale End was in being. The Revd R W Dale, a famous minister of Carrs Lane Chapel, was entirely nineteenth century, so Dale End could not have been named after him. Nearby Dalton Street had previously been the Coach Yard and the Lower Minories. The Upper Minories still exist as The Minories between Lewis's two blocks. The term 'Minories' is applied to the approach to a priory, in Birmingham's case to the — now departed — Priory of St Thomas. Dudley has 'The Minories' and it has the remains of a Cluniac Benedictine priory.

DANIELS ROAD   Bordesley Green

On the Ideal Benefit Society's 'village', and named after the Society's first General Manager, Francis William Daniels. A schoolmaster at Ebley, near Stroud, he was so impressed by George Holloway's Stroud Original Benefit

Society that after sixteen years teaching he came to Birmingham in 1891 as District Manager of the Sceptre Life Association. He felt that the Stroud idea would operate even better in an urban than a rural setting, and convinced Alderman William Kenrick of this. Thus the Ideal Benefit Society was formed, with Alderman Kenrick its President for twenty years, a period exceeded by his son Alderman Wilfred Byng Kenrick. Finnemore Road in the Ideal village is named after an early chairman of the Ideal executive committee, William Finnemore, father of Sir Donald Finnemore, the High Court judge.

DENBIGH STREET — Bordesley Green

The best-known street name connected with the Battle of Birmingham, 1643, is Camp Hill, which has even moved to Vicarage Road, Kings Heath, in the new buildings of King Edward VI (Camp Hill) School. The Ship Inn, demolished on Camp Hill, bore the legend 'Prince Rupert's Headquarters 1643'. Denbigh Street, off Bordesley Green Road, recalls the Royalist commander

who was killed in the battle. The Civil War split the Warwickshire Denbigh family. The dead earl's son, who inherited the title on his father's death, was a Parliamentary leader. In 1644 he captured the Royalist stronghold at Rushall, near Walsall. The Battle of Birmingham was fiercest around Deritend where the bladesmiths and cutlers, fervent Parliamentarians, made a spirited resistance to the Cavaliers.

DERITEND — City

It was 'a pretty streete called Dirtey' when John Leland, topographer to Henry VIII entered Birmingham from the south in 1538, finding the thoroughfare noisy with smiths, cutlers and lorimers who were to oppose Prince Rupert's Cavaliers there in 1643. Leland would have seen the Golden Lion Inn —

The original 'Ship on the Globe' trademark of Alfred Bird on Devonshire House in Deritend.

The Golden Lion Inn, originally in Deritend, now in Cannon Hill Park.

now in Cannon Hill Park — and the Old Crown Inn, built in 1348, which still survives. Near it today is Devonshire House built by Alfred Bird & Sons Ltd. of custard fame, now in Banbury. We well remember their 'Three Little Chickens' trademark, but atop Devonshire House can still be seen their earlier

The Old Crown in Deritend, Birmingham's oldest inn, dates from 1348.

trademark 'The Ship on the Globe'. On the Bull
Ring Centre opposite are two commemorative
plaques, one remembering St John's Church
thereabouts, the other John Rogers,
Birmingham's martyr, burned at the stake in
1555 by Mary Tudor.

DIGBETH City

From 'Duck's Bath', a spring at the upper end
of the thoroughfare — another spring giving
its name to Well Street (once Cook Street) off
Allison Street and parallel with Digbeth. Two
points of interest: The name MAKEPEACE can
still be seen above Key Books — once Birmingham's Moss Bros for the hire of exotic suits. On
the Digbeth corner of Park Street the Royal
George Inn shows that unfortunate ship, sunk
at Spithead in 1782 with 517 drowned, wearing
a Union Flag, correctly omitting the red diagonal cross of Ireland which was not incorporated until 1800.

*A fine model of the Royal George,
which sank off Spithead in 1782,
on a modern pub at the corner of
Park Street and Deritend.*

DOLOBRAN ROAD Sparkbrook

Dolobran is a house and estate in the Vyrnwy
valley, Montgomeryshire, and was the home of
Charles Lloyd, 1637–1698 who spent ten years
in Welshpool Gaol because he was a Quaker. In
1742 his grandson Sampson Lloyd II bought
Owen's Farm and built the Georgian mansion
'Farm', Sparkbrook, and Dolobran Road — off
Montgomery Street — formed one boundary of
Farm. In 1765 Sampson II and his son Sampson III, with John Taylor Snr and Jnr of Bordesley Hall, founded what is today Lloyds Bank.

*The Union Flag on the Royal
George. The red diagonal cross of
Ireland is absent since this was
only added in 1800.*

Camp Hill Girls sports field was in Dolobran
Road, and, on its corner with Grantham Road, Christ Church reared its spire
until losing it in a 1940 air raid.

DORA ROAD Small Heath

Small Heath had a lucky escape in coming by this simple name. The full name
of the woman it commemorates was Dora Adelaide
Featherstonehaugh-Frampton who had married Charles Wriothesley Digby of
Meriden Hall, Warwickshire, in 1881 — he was the Charles of Charles Road,
two roads from Dora Road citywards along Coventry Road. The Digbys were

a considerable family in the Coleshill area. Six Digby brothers fought on Henry VII's side at Bosworth in 1485. The family was eventually ennobled, and in 1718 Meriden Hall and land in Small Heath were left by Martyn Baldwin to an earlier Charles Wriothesley Digby, son of the 5th Lord Digby. Several Small Heath roads are named after families with which the Digbys married — Floyer, Banks, Mansell, Hugh and Somerville. There is a Digby Park. The family seat is in Dorset.

DRUIDS LANE   Druids Heath

Druids Lane was there before Druids Heath Estate was developed. While the name was a striking one it is probably a corruption of Drew. There are no Druidical connections with the area. The 1840 Kings Norton tithe Map shows West Heath, Walker's Heath and Hyter's (Highter's) Heath, but no Druids Heath — though a Mr Drew had land there, recalled in Drew's Meadow Close. Having conjured up a Druids Heath, the Public Works Department quickly hit on Stonehenge Road, following it with other Wiltshire names for roads, closes and crofts — Winterbourne, Larkhill, Bulford, Netheravon, Stapleford, Idmiston, Manningford, Baverstock. Could Pegleg Walk be another corruption — from landowner the Revd John Pegler?

DUDLEY STREET   City

Today, little more than an entrance to the bus terminus and a tunnel beneath Smallbrook Queensway, Dudley Street has an aristocratic pedigree. Birmingham's medieval Manor House was hereabouts. In 1545 the Manor of Birmingham went from the Crown to John Dudley, Lord Lisle, Lord Admiral to Henry VIII. Eight years later, John Dudley, now Duke of Northumberland, who had run England under young Edward VI, on Edward's death proclaimed his daughter-in-law Lady Jane Grey as Queen, but she, her young husband Guildford Dudley, and John Dudley himself were summarily executed by Queen Mary Tudor.

EATHORPE CLOSE   Matchborough, Redditch

Among other Warwickshire names hereabouts Eathorpe has a particular significance. It is a village on the River Leam, across which a bridge was built by 'S.S.1862'. The same initials and date appear on houses. S.S. was Samuel Shepheard who built the world-famous Shepheard's Hotel in Cairo. Born 1816, and apprenticed to a pastry-cook uncle in Leamington, Samuel ran away to sea, became a steward in a liner, fomented trouble aboard, was put ashore in Egypt with one shilling, worked in the British Hotel, Cairo — then built Shepheard's. He sold out in 1860 and retired to Eathorpe Hall as squire, died in 1866, and is buried in Wappenbury churchyard.

EBLEY ROAD
Handsworth Wood

Ebley is a Gloucestershire village near Stroud where a young schoolmaster Francis William Daniels became enthusiastic about the work of Stroud Holloway Original Benefit Society, founded in 1874 by George Holloway, MP for Mid-Gloucestershire. Daniels came to Birmingham and founded the Ideal Benefit Society (*see* Daniels Road).Its present Pitmaston offices were opened in 1931. Taking to estate building it developed among others the Cherry Orchard Estate, Handsworth Wood, where Inverclyde and Cooper Roads refer to officials of the Society.

EBRINGTON AVENUE
Solihull

(and Ebrington Gardens, Brandwood End.) From a Warwickshire village south of Ilmington Downs with a story of great significance to English history. Ebrington is the viscount's title of the earldom of the Fortescues of Ebrington Manor. Their punning motto *Forte scutum salus ducum* means 'A strong shield is the salvation of a leader'. Earl Fortescue once explained it to me — 'The first Fortescue came over with William the Conqueror and fought beside him at Hastings. During the battle Fortescue warded off with his shield an arrow which would have struck William's face'. So, but for the first Fortescue, English history could have been very different.

EDDISH ROAD
Lea Hall

Studying the *Sheldon Charities* we read of 'two fields near the Holly Fast (Hollyfaste Road) a sling in the Rye Eddish Field and the parish meadow, situate between the land of Lord Digby and Mr Taylor'. Mention is also made of a Bradford Cottage at Tyler's Cross (Tile Cross). 'Sling' occurs regularly in old documents in relation to fields, and it appears as a small road (The Sling) off Cinder Bank, Baptist End ; in Slingfield Road ; and among other field names in roads of the Wychall–West Heath area.

ELLIOTT ROAD
Selly Oak

Originally the site of the Sturgess Metal Works, established 1793. W Elliott and Son came in 1853 because of the proximity of the Worcester & Birmingham Canal, with arms into their warehouses. Selly Oak was so little developed at the time that accommodation had to be found for their workers. Elliotts was in a group with Hughes Stubbs, Muntz Metals, and Cooper and Goode, taken over by ICI (Metals) in 1928. Elliotts premises were demolished in 1928.

ERASMUS ROAD
Sparkbrook

Erasmus Road, off Stratford Road — and Darwin Street across Moseley Road in Highgate — relate to the great Galton family who lived in The Larches, near Erasmus Road, where their son who became Sir Francis Galton was born in 1822. He was the last of nine children. His mother, Violetta Darwin, was a daughter of

Dr Erasmus Darwin, grandfather of Charles Darwin of *The Origin of Species*. Two of Francis's brothers were named Erasmus and Darwin. Sir Francis Galton was an African explorer, a pioneer of eugenics, and a meteorologist who coined the term 'anti-cyclone' for a fine weather system, and published the first weather map in *The Times* on 1 April 1875. He introduced the use of fingerprints into criminology; speculated on life on Mars; and at the age of 88 wrote an unpublished Utopia called *Kantsawhere*.

ESTE ROAD   Yardley

The country home of the Lloyd banking family for 170 years. The grounds are now a public park, Farm Park.

The Este family came to Hay Hall, Tyseley, in 1423 when the last of the de la Hays, Marion, married Thomas Este, Governor of Kenilworth Castle. Hay Hall, Hay Hall Road, is the home of Reynolds Tube Co. Ltd. and has been well preserved. Some stained glass bears the initials A E—probably Anne Gibbons and Edward Este, married about 1538. The Gilbey Chapel in Yardley Church—named after another Hay Hall family—has many Este memorials. The name occurs above the baptistry in Kings Norton Church in a memorial to Sarah Este 'second wife of the late Henry Est of Slade Pool (Sladepool Farm Road) buried at Yardley in 1721'.

EUROPA AVENUE   West Bromwich

Between motorway and expressway, Europa Avenue is circular with a number of closes off it. One is Priory Close, a reminder of Sandwell Priory, founded 1130, suppressed 1526. The other closes are all named after saints including St Benedict, as the priory was Benedictine. There are St Christopher's Close; St Kenelm's Close, after the boy King of Mercia murdered in Uffmoor Wood, Clent; St Edmund's Close after a martyred King of East Anglia; St Cuthbert of Durham; and other authentic saints. But alas! — someone has blundered. Eleanor, Caroline and Augustus have been canonised by the local authority! You won't find them in the *Calendar of Saints*.

FACTORY ROAD   Handsworth

It led to Boulton's famous Soho manufactory. Born at Snow Hill, Matthew Boulton turned a small buckle factory, inherited from his father, into one of the great factories of Europe. Developing James Watt's steam power, he engaged in mass manufacturing of countless items, as well as dignified candelabra, urns and Sheffield plate. Visitors to the factory became so numerous that notices were placed in Birmingham hotels prohibiting casual visits as interfering with production. During the Priestley Riots, 1791, Boulton armed his workers against the mob. Boulton died in 1809 aged 81 and is buried in St Mary's, Handsworth.

FARMER'S BRIDGE LOCKS   City

The thirteen locks with a towpath walk which take the Birmingham Canal through the city, passing under Farmer's Bridge, once part of defunct Farmer Street. Joseph Farmer was a prosperous gun-maker who lived in prestigious Old Square, dying in 1741. His son, James, an Overseer of the Poor, moved to London in 1748 but suffered great financial loss through the 1755 Lisbon earthquake. Rehabilitating himself, he returned to Birmingham in 1765 and lived in Bingley House, dying in 1773 and commemorated in Farmer's Street name. Bingley House gave place to Bingley Hall (recently demolished to make way for the International Conference Centre), and it was visiting an exhibition of manufactures there in 1849 that inspired Prince Albert to sponsor the Great Exhibition of 1851.

FARM ROAD   Sparkbrook

The road leading from Stratford Road to 'Farm', the country home occupied by the Lloyd banking family for 170 years. Sampson Lloyd II purchased Owen's Farm of 56 acres, with a Tudor farmhouse, on 28 April 1742 for £1,290. In 1745 he planted a fine avenue of trees leading to the site of the splendid Georgian house 'Farm' which he built four years later. At one time 'Farm' became a Sons of Rest headquarters, and its grounds have been a public park and adventure playground since the 1920s.

FARNOL ROAD   Yardley

After Jeffrey Farnol, author, born at Aston, Birmingham, in 1878; its neighbour Vibart Road after one of his characters. His novels of Corinthian life were avidly read between the wars, *The Amateur Gentleman*, *The Broad Highway*, and *The Hon. Mr Tawnish* among the most popular. Farnol lived in New York from 1902 to 1910, published stories in magazines, and for two years painted scenery at the Astor Theatre, New York. He died in 1952 at Eastbourne, and has a splendidly sited memorial seat at Wilmington facing the chalk figure of The Long Man of Wilmington on the Sussex Downs.

FASHODA ROAD Selly Park

Off Dogpool Lane, parallel with Pershore Road, it has more of that road's 'Alphabet Houses'. On one side twenty-four houses begin with a letter each from Amberley (Glos.) to Yapton (Sussex). Its three neighbouring roads, Kitchener, Cecil and Manilla, with Fashoda Road, constitute a dated development. In July 1898 General Kitchener confronted a French expedition under the French explorer Colonel Marchand at a remote village, Fashoda, on the

One of the attractively decorated signs on the 'Alphabet Houses' in Pershore Road.

Upper Nile, in an explosive incident which was settled by the good sense of Robert Cecil, Lord Salisbury, the Foreign Minister. But what of the stranger in the quartet, Manilla? Also in 1898 on 1 May the US fleet destroyed the Spanish fleet at Manilla Bay in the Philippines. So this building development obviously occurred while these two events were in the mind.

FATHERLESS BARN CRESCENT Halesowen

'Can you throw light on the Fatherless Barn district of Halesowen?', a reader of the *Streetwise* column in the Evening Mail asked. So I find a Fatherless Barn Crescent west of Drew's Holloway. Locals tell, predictably, of 'some murder' in a barn. One believed that Halesowen Abbey had a barn there with a Father Lees the custodian. Now to fact: I possess an auctioneer's Notice of Sale in 1874 of Mineral Property around 'The Township of Luttley' incorporating a map showing 'Fatherless Barn, Harper and Moore' on the site of the present crescent. Other items on the map are collieries: J Fisher's; Hickman's; King Bros; Holcrofts (Holcroft Road today); and another Harper and Moore. Around 1914 Francis Brett Young in his book *Cold Harbour* introduced a fictional Fatherless Bairn Colliery and a Sedgebury Main Colliery, both based on the actual Two Gates Colliery (Two Gates Lane).

FENTHAM ROAD

Off Gravelly Hill North, and elsewhere in Birmingham and Solihull. George Fentham, born 1630 at Hampton-in-Arden, died 1698. A country boy became a rich Birmingham mercer. He dug clay for bricks in Moor Street for the Roman Catholic chapel and priest's house in Masshouse Lane — *'Franciscan Register 1688: Mr George Fentham gave in bricks (who is a Protestant) £15'*. He left £30 annuity to Hampton poor, and £10 to supply ten coats to ten poor widows dwelling within 200 yds of the Bull Ring. By his charity children within 200 yds of the Bull Ring were taught to read, and children of both sexes were provided for at Birmingham Blue Coat School 'wearing however green coats instead of blue to distinguish them'.

FITZROY AVENUE   Harborne

It was from the marriage of the Fourth Lord Calthorpe to a daughter of the Duke of Beaufort that one of their forenames, Fitzroy, came to a branch of the Calthorpes — all the Dukes of Beaufort have Fitzroy in their name. The same Calthorpe branch gives its name to Hamilton Road from one of its forenames. Balden Road, Harborne, is named after E H Balden, a Calthorpe estate agent up to the mid-1920s. Blakeney Avenue is a place-name in the Calthorpe's Norfolk territory.

FOLLIOTT ROAD   Lea Hall

Among Yardley Charities 'Aylmer Folliott directed his trustees to convey a cottage and certain lands which were divided into three closes between Yardley Church and Lyme Green (Lyme Green Road), for the use of the poor of the parish'. Reference is also made to the rent of land at Smart's Hill, Aylmer Folliott's gift, and a property called Deepmoores (Deepmoor Road) purchased for use of the poor by donations totalling £26. William Flakeleye in the 1327 subsidy rolls, and three fields, The Flaxleys, on the 1847 enclosure map, account for Flaxley Road.

FORD STREET   Hockley

Near Hockley Circus. About 1779 Richard Ford built 'Hockley Abbey' (Abbey Street), a folly, of slag from Aston Furnace and worked the date 1473 in small pebbles on to the frontage as a false suggestion of antiquity. When ivy-clad it did look ancient. Ford claimed to have built his 'abbey' on the same money that his workers spent on ale — two shillings a day. An ingenious eccentric, he constructed a one-wheel carriage for which the Society of Arts presented him with their gold medal.

FORMANS ROAD   Sparkhill

It was known in medieval times as Foulsmoreslone. It had become Folmur Lane in 1562. These names arose from the 'foul ford' where the River Cole crossed the Stratford Road. A family of Fulfords also took their name from the ford where, in 1275, one of the family, Roger Fullard, was drowned. Their home was Fulford Hall which became Grove Farm on the spring-line between the marl and the drift, demolished in 1897 but leaving us Grove Road in Sparkhill. Around 1900 the Cole bridge in Formans Road replaced a wooden one known as 'Formers'. Hereabouts the Small Heath tornado of 14 June 1931 started, killing one woman in Formans Road.

FOX HOLLIES ROAD   Hall Green

A widespread name — I used a Forces Canteen in Fox Hollies Road, Seaford, Sussex in 1944. Maps in hunting country show copses called Fox Hollies. Walmley has a Fox Hollies Road, Fox Covert and Holly Lane. The Hall Green street map has Fox Green Crescent and Fox Grove, names not from hunting but from a Fox family who appeared thereabouts in 1465 and purchased a farm from the Atte Hollies family — who got their name from living near holly bushes. By 1624 the farm was called Foxholleys. Tower blocks in Curtis Gardens, Holly Piece, Home Meadow, and Coppice, are named from fields on Fox Hollies Hall Estate of that late picturesque character, Colonel Zaccheus Walker.

FREER ROAD   Birchfield

The Freers were considerable landowners in the city, best known for Canon Freer's part in Birmingham becoming a diocese. In 1836 St Philip's Parish Church was transferred from Coventry and Lichfield diocese to Worcester. In 1888 the Bishop of Worcester suggested Birmingham became a separate ecclesiastical entity. With Dr Charles Gore becoming Bishop of Worcester in 1902 the possibility of a Birmingham diocese was again discussed, and in a letter to *The Times* Canon Freer offered £10,000 towards this. Gore matched this with his own £10,000 plus £800 annually from his Worcester stipend. In 1904 Joseph Chamberlain successfully sponsored a Birmingham Bishopric Bill which became law. Dr Gore was enthroned as Birmingham's first bishop in 1905.

FREETH STREET   Ladywood

John Freeth was Birmingham's ballad-monger. Born 1731, he was apprenticed to a Park Street brassfounder. In 1768 he took over from his mother Freeth's Coffee House, Bell Street, otherwise the Leicester Arms, which enshrined 'the history of popular political consciousness in Birmingham'. A Book Club met there. Freeth celebrated the arrival of coals by the newly constructed Birmingham Canal: 'For true-feeling joy in each breast must be wrought, When coals under fivepence per hundred are bought'. His poem against taxes during the American War of Independence might find echoes today: 'For taxes we find ere the work is half finished, Have increased, are increasing, and should be diminished'.

GARBETT STREET   Spring Hill

Let *Streetwise* recall the name of a great Brummie rudely erased from street
nomenclature by housing development just off Sandpits. Samuel Garbett
(1717–1803), merchant, and partner in Carron Ironworks, active in many
aspects of the town — The Birmingham Library; General Hospital (and the
Triennial Music Festivals which helped finance it); canals; the Magistracy. In
1785, with Josiah Wedgwood of the pottery, he formed the national
protectionist General Chamber of Manufacturers. He advocated dividing
Crown Forests into agricultural holdings. A friend of most members of the
Lunar Society though not one himself.

GARRISON LANE   Small Heath

When the Priestley Riots were at their height in Birmingham in 1791, two
troops of the 15th Regiment of Dragoons were called to make a forced march
from Nottingham to quell the reign of terror. As was the custom in those days
they were billeted in pubs and private houses to the annoyance of publicans
and residents. So it was decided to construct a barracks on four acres of land
at Ashted, the first stone being laid in August 1792. Thus the 4th Dragoons
were at hand to put down the Chartist Riots in Birmingham in 1839. The
barrack area was developed around Garrison Lane with military sounding
streets — Camp Street, Artillery Street, Barracks Street; and Wolseley Street
and Gordon Street named after generals. The area is now demilitarised.

GEM STREET   Gosta Green

"I'm making a scrap-book of *Streetwise* to pass to my grandchildren", wrote a
Shirley *Evening Mail* reader. "There aren't many of our old streets left now".

A minor menagerie disappeared under the College of Technology, later
Aston University (1966) — Buck, Doe, Fox, Sheep and Bullock streets. Gem
Street went too, named after Thomas Gem, an attorney, secretary to the
Trustees of the Bromsgrove and Birmingham Turnpike, and in September 1792
elected secretary of the Bean Club, which still exists. It was founded after the
Restoration of Charles II in 1688 as a loyalist drinking club where gentlemen
from country districts could meet with important townsmen to their mutual
advantage.

GIBBONS HILL ROAD   Sedgley

The Gibbons family once occupied Ellowes Hall, Sedgley. They were in
business and ironmasters in 1720. In 1824 Benjamin Gibbons discovered
high-grade fireclay on his property and founded the firm of B Gibbons Jnr,
forerunner of Gibbons (Dudley) Ltd, to manufacture fireclay goods for the new
gas industry. Cuba Pit, now closed, was so named because fireclay was first
mined there — at Lower Gornal — on the day in 1898 that the US–Spanish War
ended in Cuba.

GILBERTSTONE AVENUE   Yardley

The Gilbertstone is one of several boulders in the Birmingham area brought down in the ice sheet from North Wales — others being in Cannon Hill Park, Olton Park, and at The Gutter, south of Clent. With road development in 1937 the Gilbertstone was placed near the junction of Coventry, Beechmore and Brays Roads — not far from the junction of Gilbertstone Avenue with the Coventry Road but on the opposite side. In 1952 it was removed to Lyndon Green Junior School, and in 1978 to Blakesley Hall Museum, Yardley, where it can be seen in the herb garden. Legend has it that a giant named Gilbert placed the stone where in 1609 the parishes of Yardley, Bickenhill and Elmdon met.

GILLOTT ROAD   Edgbaston

During the post-Waterloo slump, Joseph Gillott, an apprentice scissors-grinder, came from Sheffield and found work in Birmingham stamping buckles by a new process. His girl-friend was the sister of pen manufacturers William and John Mitchell, and Joseph applied his buckle-stamping process to pen-nibs, making a gross on his wedding morning and selling them for one shilling each to his guests. He prospered, had accounts in each Birmingham bank, built his own works at Hockley, bought Rotton Park Estate, became an art collector, produced costly gems casually from his pockets, owned six Stradivarius violins, and on his death in 1872 his art collection raised £164,530 at Christies.

GLOUCESTER STREET   City

Off Edgbaston Street in the market area — included here for a tradition still operating there in the 1950s. In a sorting yard in Gloucester Street early each morning a police sergeant was surrounded by cloth-capped barrow-boys. He drew numbered discs from a bag corresponding to the licence numbers of the hawkers, shouting them like a bingo caller. First out would get the plum barrow position on Bell Street corner, the next twenty-nine coming in order down Spiceal Street to the poorest position on Edgbaston Street corner. Then followed a stampede for forty places in Jamaica Row. There were great market characters — Charlie Morgan, Jimmy Phillips, Jack Orme, Billy Connor, the Moseleys and Chapmans.

GOLDEN HILLOCK ROAD   Small Heath

Golden Hillock was a field name on a 1760 tithe map. Golden Hillock Farm was near the corner of Cooksey Road and Golden Hillock Road. It was earlier Danford Farm, and the road itself Danford Lane. In 1763 the farm was advertised 'to be let as Sylvester's Farm near the Golden Hillock'. The recent island on the Small Heath Highway – Golden Hillock Road crossing is called Poet's Corner after nearby Byron, Tennyson and Waverley (Sir Walter Scott) Roads

GOTHIC SUBWAY

City

Birmingham's underpass names tend to go unnoticed. This one, off St Chad's Circus, gets mention because, regretting the demise of old street names, one remembers Gothic Arcade, off Snow Hill. Gothic Subway is practically on its site, its name springing from the Gothic architecture of St Chad's Cathedral, built in 1839–41, the first Roman Catholic cathedral built in England after the Reformation. Its architect, Augustus Welby Northmore Pugin, remembered in Pugin Subway, was the great neo--Gothic enthusiast. He said 'There is nothing worth living for but Christian architecture and a boat'. He went about his daily business, designing neo-Gothic churches, dressed as a ship's pilot.

GOUGH STREET

Edgbaston

Harry Gough had a 25-acre farm where Gough Street now runs into Suffolk Street Queensway. He was one of sixteen children of Sir Henry Gough, a wealthy Wolverhampton wool merchant who came to Perry Hall in 1669. Henry's younger brother, Sir Richard, was an eminent East India merchant, and on one of his journeys to China and India he took the 11-year-old Harry as his secretary. Young Harry himself prospered in the East, and with the farm he also bought part of the Middlemore Estate in Birmingham. Sir Harry's Road, Edgbaston, is named after Harry's cousin, another Sir Henry Gough. The Gough crest, a

The boar's head weather vane on St Philip's Cathedral recognises Sir Henry Gough's assistance in obtaining royal funding towards the building.

The acknowledgement of Sir Henry Gough's help in St Philip's Cathedral.

boar's head, is the wind-vane of St Philip's Cathedral, Sir Richard Gough having prevailed on George I to give £600 towards the building of the tower.

GRAHAM STREET
Hockley

Named after one of Wellington's generals who fought at Vittoria in 1819 — Vittoria Street runs off Graham Street. On Graham Street corner with Frederick Street in 1816 was the home of Alderman Van Wart, and staying there was his wife's brother, the American writer Washington Irving, despondent because literary inspiration was eluding him. One evening an idea struck Irving. He stayed up all night writing, and when the Van Warts came down to breakfast he read to them the draft of his famous story *Rip Van Winkle*. Later the house became the offices of Joseph Gillott's pen works, which he built in Frederick Street with an enormous ship's mast protruding through the roof as a flagpole.

GRANVILLE STREET
off Broad Street

There are Earls Granville associated with Stone, Staffordshire. Sir George Granville, a Staffordshire MP, was private secretary to Prime Minister Gladstone 1880–85. A branch of the family lived at Wellesbourne Hall, Warwickshire, and there is a Granville Arms pub at Barford. In 1876 the Birmingham West Suburban Railway opened from Granville Street to a junction with the Gloucester line at Kings Norton, via Church Road, Somerset Road, Selly Oak, and Stirchley stations. In 1885 the line was extended to New Street and the Granville Street terminus was replaced by Five Ways Station.

GREAT COLMORE STREET
Lee Bank

The original entrance towards Birmingham's market area from Worcestershire was down Holloway Head. To ease congestion New Road was constructed through the Colmore's Bell Barn Estate and alongside the notorious area of Green's Village, eventually obliterated by John Bright Street. This New Road was renamed Great Colmore Street. St Asaph's Church (1868) has gone without trace from the angle of Great Colmore and Latimer Street. In 1918 William Barwick Cregoe-Colmore sold much of his Bell Barn Estate on terms favourable to the tenants.

GREAT LISTER STREET
Ashted

Sir Lister Holte of the Aston Hall Holtes leased land to Dr John Ash, a founder and first senior physician of the General Hospital — thus Great Lister Street, Ashted Row, and the district Ashted. Dr Ash built a sumptuous house on the land. When he left for London the house was converted into St James's Church (now demolished), and his estate developed as a fashionable suburb by John Brooke, an attorney, who took over Dr Ash's lease and whose name is perpetuated in Great Brooke Street. William Hutton wrote of 'worthy Dr Ash who in 1788 saved my life, and who by skill and assiduity acquired £25,000'.

GREAT STONE ROAD   Northfield

The Great Stone Inn is not in this road but in Church Road nearby. The inn's gimmick was the claim that 'Beer is Sold by the Stone', for in the ancient pound is Northfield's 'Great Stone' — an erratic glacial boulder carried down from the Arenig Mountains, North Wales, in the ice sheet. Other glacial boulders are in Cannon Hill Park, Olton Park, the Gilbertstone at Yardley

which gives its name to Gilbertstone Avenue, the War Stone at Hockley from which Warstone Lane derives, one at Solihull, and one at Bell Heath south of the Lickeys.

The ancient pound in Northfield, originally used for confiscating stray cattle, now the home of the 'Great Stone'.

GREET MILL HILL   Hall Green

You won't find this name in the A to Z, but it is popularly given to the hill rising from the Cole bridge to York Road on Stratford Road. Mysterious because Greet is on the Warwick Road around the River Cole. Yet Greet Mill stood at the ford where Stratford Road crossed the river, the last mill on the site being demolished in 1855. When the bridge was built in 1913 remains of the mill and mill stream were found. A plan to join the Worcester Canal with the Grand Union by canalizing the Cole never materialised.

GUY'S CLOSE Tamworth

Thomas Guy, founder of Guy's Hospital, London, and builder of Tamworth Town Hall, was MP for Tamworth. He also built the almshouses in Lower Gungate, but his charitable nature could not withstand the shock of defeat in a parliamentary election in 1707, and he refused any place in the almshouses to his ungrateful constituents. Peel Rise commemorates the Peel family of Drayton Bassett. Sir Robert Peel represented Tamworth in the House of Commons from 1837 to 1850, was twice Prime Minister, and died in 1850 of injuries after falling from his horse.

HADZOR ROAD Warley

Samuel Galton Jnr, banker and gunsmith, bought Warley estate for £7,300. His son Hubert built the Gothic Warley Abbey, demolished in 1957. Hadzor House, near Droitwich, built for the Amphletts around 1702, had been the seat of this branch of the Galtons since 1821. The Hadzor Galtons were Roman Catholics. Theodore Howard Galton built a Catholic church at Hadzor, opened in 1878. His son, Major Hugh Galton of Hadzor House, lost his two sons in the 1914 War. He died in 1928, and in 1930 the Society of the Divine Word came to Hadzor House and it continued as a Roman Catholic seminary.

HALLAM STREET West Bromwich

The street, and the Hallam Hospital, are named after the family of the great historian Henry Hallam, author of *The Constitutional History of England* who inherited from his father the now-demolished Charlemont Hall (Charlemont Road and Estate). Henry married the daughter of the Revd Sir Abraham Elton, Vicar of West Bromwich 1782–90, and their son became a great friend of the poet Alfred, Lord Tennyson. He was the 'A H H' of Tennyson's famous poem *In Memoriam* which runs to 131 stanzas.

HAMLET ROAD Hall Green

Not Shakespeare. Merely the road leading off Stratford Road to the hamlet of Hall Green centred around Job Marston's Chapel and Hawe Green House which stood between what are now Fox Hollies and Studland Roads. The growth of Birmingham assimilating outlying communities is underlined by a memorial in Holy Trinity Church, Camp Hill, describing John Simcox, died 1837, as 'a native of this hamlet' — Bordesley. A hamlet called Tenchlee has become Acocks Green. Greet and Yardley were hamlets eventually drawn into Birmingham.

HAMS ROAD Saltley

Hams Road is off Adderley Road, named after the family which built Hams Hall at Lea Marston, now the site of the power station. The hall was bought after the First World War by Oswald Harrison, a shipping magnate, and rebuilt at Coates, near Cirencester, called Bledisloe Lodge after Viscount Bledisloe, one-time chairman of the college governors and a Governor General of New Zealand. In 1849 at Hams Hall, Lea Marston, Charles Bowyer Adderley (the first Lord Norton) as Under-Secretary for the Colonies, prepared a constitution for New Zealand, still known as the Hams Draft. So Hams Hall Power Station inherited its name from an actual Hams Hall, the name remaining in this little road in the Adderley territory.

HANNON ROAD Alcester Lanes End

From 1922 to 1945 Moseley parliamentary constituency was represented by Sir Patrick Hannon, Conservative, whose dwindling majority underlined the decline in his party's fortunes in Birmingham. Unopposed in 1922, then with a majority of 26,000 in 1935 decreasing to 993 in 1945, after which the constituency disappeared. Moseley first appeared as a constituency in 1918, won for the Conservatives with a majority of 12,372 by Sir Hallewell Rogers.

HANSOM ROAD Quinton

In a group of 'discoverers and inventors' road names. J A Hansom was designer of the Hansom cab and, with his partner E Welch, of Birmingham Town Hall, begun in 1832. The other roads: Arkwright Road (Richard Arkwright, water frame spinning); Pitman Road (Isaac Pitman, shorthand); Plimsoll Road (Samuel Plimsoll, ship's loading line); Wedgwood Road (Josiah Wedgwood, pottery); Faraday Road (Michael Faraday, electricity); Fleming Road (Alexander Fleming, penicillin). An *Evening Mail* reader from Hansom Road asked about nearby Ridgacre Road. From the proximity of Upper Meadow Road and Middle Meadow Avenue it seems to be one of those natural features/field name/farm name group of roads.

HARMAN ROAD Sutton Coldfield

Sutton has a Vesey Road, so obviously named after Bishop Vesey that everyone knows it. It is less well known that the great ecclesiastic who gave Sutton Park to the people was often described as Harman alias Vesey. He was born John Harman in 1452, his father a Sutton yeoman who died when John was eight. Brought up by his uncle Vesey, John assumed his name. He was tutor to Mary Tudor, friend of her father Henry VIII, and Bishop of Exeter. Retiring to Sutton he introduced kersey[1] weaving, built fifty-one houses for weavers, and Moor Hall for himself where he lived like a potentate with 150 liveried servants. He paved Sutton streets and built bridges. He died in 1555 aged 103 and is buried in Sutton Parish Church.

HARTOPP ROAD   Sutton Coldfield

Fringes the site of Four Oaks Park, once the home of Sir Edmund Hartopp who, from the Sutton Enclosure Act of 1825, gained the freehold of part of 3,500 acres of common land previously belonging to the community. In 1826 Hartopp wanted to add sixty-three picturesque acres called Ladywood to his park, and in exchange offered Sutton Corporation ninety-three acres, mainly meadow, adjacent to Town and Boldmere gates. He also offered to create a direct road — now Park Road — from Mill Street to the park, previous entry having been via Manor Hill and Wyndley Pool.

HAVERGAL WALK   Halesowen

Frances Ridley Havergal, the hymn writer, was born at Astley, Worcestershire near Stourport in 1838, and is buried in Astley churchyard. She wrote 'Who is on the Lord's side?', 'Thy life was given for me' and other hymns. Her father, the Revd William Havergal, composed hymn tunes. But now from the sacred to the secular — off Havergal Walk is Whynot Street. Can this have the same origin as *Why Not?* pubs? *Why Not?* was a bay gelding out of Twitter by Castlereagh, winner of the Grand National 1894 and fifty-two other races. The sign of the *Why Not?* pub at Astwood Bank, Redditch shows a horseshoe surrounding a horse's head.

HEATH MILL LANE   Deritend

One of the mills on the River Rea — a corn mill owned by a Mr Cooper in 1756, when he claimed to have lost one guinea an hour through flooding when Duddeston Mill downstream failed to raise the sluices. Off Heath Mill Lane, visible across the forecourt of Deritend Service Station, is a mysterious campanile on a church-like building. This was built privately by the Revd John Lopes, a Church of England clergyman of St Basil's, Heath Mill Lane, as St Edmunds Hostel and Chapel for Working Boys in 1915–16. Father Lopes joined the Roman Catholic Church and handed the building to the Sisters of St Vincent de Paul who used the hostel for Irish girls working on munitions in Birmingham. When the Sisters left it became a store for chinaware.

---

1   a coarse woollen cloth

HEATON STREET   Hockley

Near the Birmingham Mint, Icknield Street, and named after the Heaton family. The first Ralph Heaton in a dynasty of five founded a brassfoundry firm in Shadwell Street in 1794. In 1889 this became The Mint (Birmingham) Ltd. Prior to that, as Ralph Heaton and Sons Ltd, it had in 1853 begun making copper coins for the Royal Mint, such coins being identified by an H beneath the date of the old pennies and halfpennies. K.N. in that position means the coin was made at Kings Norton Mint. Apprenticed to Ralph Heaton in 1864, Edward Wyon in 1881 went for Heaton's to establish Columbia's Mint at Bogota. In 1888 when Heaton's set up China's Imperial Mint at Canton, Wyon took skilled men from Heaton's on the job. He stayed on in China as chief of the Operations Department of the Mint.

HEMLINGFORD ROAD   Shard End

The four 'hundreds' of Warwickshire are Barlichway, Kington, Knightlow, and Hemlingford which embraces Birmingham. A 'hundred' was a Saxon local government area of 100 'hides' of land ranging from 60 to 120 acres a hide. The hundred has no relevance today except in an archaic survival as a 'leet' which was a lesser form of local government. Today Court Leets exist at Bromsgrove, Henley-in-Arden and Alcester, with bailiffs, ale-tasters, brook-lookers, etc. elected annually — socially prestigious officers without powers.

HENN STREET   City

Once off Bull Street, but now gone, as has Henn's Walk (see under Moor Street). Mr John Henn asked could I tell him any more about the Henn family. I was able to mention Isaac Henn, wood-screw and nail maker and factor of Park Street (*Wrightsons's Triennial Directory, 1818*). Mr Henn told me of Henry Henn, merchant of Bull Street, near Henn Street. He also mentioned his father referring to a pub in Milk Street, Deritend, where all the regulars were Henns. John thereupon went to an old census and discovered six prolific families of Henns in Barn Street, the continuation of Milk Street.

HENSHAW ROAD   Small Heath

Frederick Henry Henshaw was an artist, born in Birmingham 1807, who lived in Green Lane, Small Heath, and died in 1891, still painting at eighty-four. For some years he was secretary to Birmingham Royal Society of Artists. Under Turner's influence Henshaw mainly portrayed nature, most effectively in woodland scenes. He exhibited in London and Birmingham from 1826 onwards. In 1866 he had a special display of 200 of his works in Birmingham Art Gallery. Today the Gallery has his *Study of a Barn and Trees*; *Study of Cornfields*; and *An Old Cottage near Thames Ditton, Surrey*.

HIGH STREET   Harborne

Tom Presterne, local historian, dates the break-up of rural Harborne from the development of three neighbouring streets off High Street. Named after the landowner they were Josiah, Bull, and York Streets, though Josiah has since become South Street. The Green Man in High Street was the headquarters of the Harborne Gooseberry Growers Society, founded in 1815 by schoolmaster Thomas Baker and spectacle maker James Barton. Another spectacle maker, Emmanuel Withers, once won sixteen out of seventeen classes at Stone, Staffordshire — the deadly rival gooseberry centre! — including the heaviest dozen at 15¾ ounces.

HILL HOOK ROAD   Sutton Coldfield

There was a Hill Hook Farm. Now there are, in Clarence Road nearby, two blocks of flats, Hill Hook House and Bickley house — a family named Bickley once lived at the farm. In the exterior wall of Hill Hook House is the 'Bickley Stone', formerly in the farmhouse wall. It is inscribed: 'Here on the First of August 1797 John Bickley and the horse he rode were struck dead by lightning. Happily he was an amiable youth. Be ye also ready. Matt. 22: 44'. One supposes that John's amiability enabled him to accept his demise gracefully instead of being annoyed at the inconvenience. The Bickley Stone, on a recent visit, was, unfortunately, no longer visible, having been covered by a board.

HINGESTON STREET   Hockley

Recent discussion concerning a possible Asian name for a street is a reminder that some twenty years ago, before redevelopment, Hingeston Street, off Icknield Street, would have felt like home to Birmingham's immigrants from the Indian sub-continent. Its 'places' — courts — bore concrete name-tablets inspired by the Indian Mutiny of 1857: Poonamallee 1866; Rajahkistnapooram 1867; Baulchettychoultry and Streepematoor 1868; Serringapottam and Trichernoppelly 1870. There were also captains and campaigns — Napier Place; Abyssinia Place; and Christian's Buildings, Corbett's Buildings; and Poor Robin's Cottage.

HOLDER ROAD   Hay Mills

Off Coventry Road, and named after Sir John Holder, a brewer. Also off Coventry Road and running into Deakins Road immediately downhill of Holder Road are Kathleen, Geraldine, Flora and Gladys Roads, named after Sir John's daughters. He owned land in the area but lived in a house at Pitmaston, above Cannon Hill Park, acquired after his death in 1923 by the Ideal Benefit Society who demolished it and built their attractive present offices on the site. At Pitmaston he is remembered in Sir John's Road and Holders Lane. Sir John was a great civic benefactor. On Boxing Day 1906 he declared open St Andrew's football ground — on a derelict area acquired for

£10,000 by Birmingham Football Club (not yet Birmingham City). The First Division match against Middlesborough ended in a goal-less draw, the start being delayed until 12 noon while fifty men cleared several inches of snow off the pitch. The attendance was 32,000.

HOLLOWAY HEAD   Lee Bank

The old entry to Birmingham worn hollow by traffic trundling downhill to busy Smallbrook Street. Off Holloway Head was Speaking Stile Walk, so called from an echo there, and Windmill Street which once had a tower windmill. Holloway Head's place in history comes from its having been — with Newhall Hill — Birmingham's great outdoor meeting place earlier last century. In August 1838 a gathering of 100,000 people in Holloway Head adopted the National Petition embodying the Six Points of the People's Charter, five of which have become law. In 1839 the Chartist Convention with militant leaders moved into Birmingham, and on 16 July, as Chartists massed in Holloway Head, police and Dragoons were called, and the Riot Act read.

HOWE STREET   Duddeston

Lady Sophia Howe, eldest daughter of Admiral Earl Howe, was the niece of Charles Jennens ('Solyman the Magnificent' — *see* Jennens Road) who owned territory in the Duddeston area. She married the Hon. Penn Assheton Curzon in 1787, and they inherited most of the Jennens Estate (Penn Street, Curzon Street). Admiral Howe's best-known naval victory was 'The Glorious First of June' 1794, against the French in mid-Atlantic. He also settled the notorious Spithead Mutiny in 1797. The 5th Earl Howe was a famous racing motorist between the wars. Until its demolition in 1951–2 the Howes lived in Jennens's grandiose Gopsall Hall, Leicestershire, and have memorials in Congerstone Church nearby.

HUTTON ROAD   Saltley

Derby-born William Hutton, Birmingham's first historian, settled here as a bookseller in High Street in 1750, opened Birmingham's first circulating library in 1751, and in 1756 the first paper warehouse. He became a Commissioner for the recovery of debts and built Red Hill House on Washwood Heath Road, damaged in the Priestley Riots, 1791. His son built Bennetts Hill House opposite — hence Bennetts Road as well as Hutton Road today. William Hutton published his *History of Birmingham* in 1782 very successfully. He also farmed at Stechford, and at 82 could walk 40 miles in a day. He died in 1815 aged 92, and is buried at Aston Parish Church. St Margaret's Church, Ward End, has a bust and memorial.

HYPERION ROAD   Bromford

Off Bromford Drive, which is named after Birmingham's old Bromford Bridge Racecourse, is one of a group of roads named after famous racehorses.

Hyperion won the 1933 Derby and St Leger, and sired eleven winners of classic races. Papyrus Way remembers Papyrus, the 1923 Derby winner and Steve Donoghue's third Derby winner. Reynoldstown Road recalls the winner of the 1935 and 1936 Grand Nationals; and can Tipperary Close commemorate any other horse than Tipperary Tim, the 100 to 1 Grand National winner in 1928? Trigo and Ayala Crofts are also named after racehorses. Cremorne Road, Sutton Coldfield recalls the 1872 Derby winner, who is buried in Rufford Abbey, Nottinghamshire.

ICKNIELD STREET   Hockley

Part of the main route of the Roman Icknield or Ryknield Street. It comes from the south via Beoley, the foot of Weatheroak Hill, Forhill, and enters Birmingham around Kings Norton. Its route continuing northward through the city including Icknield Street, proceeds through Sutton Park, much in its original state, above Longmoor Pool, past Rowton Well, and leaves the park at Streetly (the Icknield 'street'), passes through Little Aston as Roman Road, and so to Wall, the Roman legion's staging post of Letocetum, near Lichfield. Birmingham's Icknield Street has The Birmingham Mint and Key Hill Cemetery.

INGE STREET   City

Inge Street and Thorp Street, off Hurst Street, are named after the wealthy Inge family once of Thorpe Hall, Thorpe Constantine, Staffordshire. Thorp Street was noted for its drill hall from which countless Brummies marched to war. Inge Street was the birthplace, in 1817, of George Jacob Holyoake, social reformer and Co-operative pioneer. In his autobiography Holyoake writes of Inge Street as a 'glorious glen' during his boyhood, with the Fox Tavern then — as now — on Hurst Street corner. Later in his long life — he died in 1906 — Holyoake wrote that looking from the Horse Fair and Inge Street was like 'the entrance to a coal-pit'.

IZON ROAD   West Bromwich

In a Directory of 1770 John Izon is entered as a hinge-maker of Coleshill Street, Birmingham. In 1775 a patent for a secret hinge was granted to John Izon and Thomas Whitehurst, brass-founders of Duke Street, Birmingham. In response to a *Birmingham Gazette* advertisement of 1782 Izon and Whitehurst took the lease of Greet's Mill on the River Tame at West Bromwich where they established a foundry, adapting the machinery of the corn mill to producing hardware. The water power proving inadequate, a Boulton and Watt steam engine was installed and the foundry became just Izons — today Izon and Co. Ltd. The old mill house was demolished in 1941.

JENNENS ROAD City

Off Masshouse Circus. Charles Jennens, after whose family the road is named, was a friend of Handel who revised his *Messiah* on the organ at Gopsall Hall, Charles's great Leicestershire mansion — now demolished — while Jennens himself arranged the Biblical libretto of *Messiah*. Charles's father had a Queen Anne town house in High Street where now the Pavilions stands; and iron furnaces at Bromford, near his country home, Erdington Hall; at Aston — hence Furnace Lane there — and at Furnace End beyond Shustoke. Charles was known as 'Solyman the Magnificent' from his ostentation, travelling by coach and four with four cockaded footmen. He died a bachelor in 1773 and is buried at Nether Whitacre.

JENKINS STREET Small Heath

In the 1880s a frontage along Coventry Road in Small Heath consisted of a parcel of arable land known as Small Heath Meadow, and two others known as Small Heath Fields. In 1845 the Aston Tithe Map described them as owned by John Jenkins and occupied by Henry Jenkins after which family the road through one of them was named. Jenkins Street School was renamed Goodwin School after a long-serving headmaster of that name earlier this century. He retired to Temple Grafton where he lived to pass his century.

JESSON ROAD Sutton Coldfield

Named after Thomas Jesson, a silk mercer, who in April 1707 founded the Jesson Charity for 'apprenticing children of Sutton Coldfield and granting assistance to young people towards their education, studies, and advancement in life'. Jesson also gave £2 per annum for distribution of bread on St Thomas's Day to the poor attending Holy Trinity Church. In 1697 Sutton Corporation granted the Lyndrich (Lindridge) Pools to W Jesson of Langley at a rent of three shillings and six bottles of wine to the warden. Lingard Road and Fowler Road nearby are named after Frances Lingard who endowed almshouses, and Clara Fowler whose charity, along with those of Jesson and Lingard, is now administered by Sutton Coldfield Municipal Charities.

JOHN BRIGHT STREET City

John Bright, born at Rochdale, Lancashire, of Quaker stock, was a Liberal MP for Birmingham from 1857 until his death in 1889, though he had earlier represented another constituency from 1843. Best known for his campaign — with Richard Cobden — for the repeal of the Corn Laws. Their Anti-Corn Law League believed that Britain's refusal to buy foreign corn injured home trade because food was so dear that people had no money to spend on other goods — and that foreign corn producers would not buy our manufactures. Bright's other campaign for the extension of the franchise helped bring in the Reform

Act of 1867. From 1868 to 1880 Bright held office in Liberal governments, eventually resigning from his opposition to government policy on Egypt.

KEDLESTON ROAD Hall Green

Among a group with Derbyshire place-names — Etwall, Dalbury, Doveridge and Eggington — Kedleston Road has the most aristocratic pedigree. Of the 1st Marquess Curzon of Kedleston it was written 'My name is George Nathaniel Curzon; I am a most superior person'. Kedleston Hall is the most splendid Georgian house in Derbyshire. Among other offices George Nathaniel was Viceroy of India 1898–1905; Foreign Secretary 1919–1924; and leader of the House of Lords. He might have become Prime Minister instead of Baldwin in March 1923 on Bonar Law's resignation. The family had connections with Curzon Street, Birmingham.

KEEL DRIVE Hall Green

A cul-de-sac off Green Road that reminds me of sharks. I know its origin is Irish because two other names offered by developers and rejected by the Public Works Committee some thirty years ago were Tara ('the harp that once . . .') and, astonishingly, Croke Park, the Dublin sports stadium, scene of a massacre on 21 November 1920 by British Auxiliaries. Keel is a small community on Achill Island off the west coast of Ireland and, when I visited it, the headquarters of a shark industry by local fishermen, whose look-out on Meenawn cliffs sent the boats in search of tell-tale fins.

KENRICK WAY West Bromwich

When shoe buckles gave place to laces Archibald Kenrick moved his buckle business from Birmingham to West Bromwich in 1791, making flat irons and humane mantraps etc. in Spon Lane. His sons, Archibald jun. and Timothy joined him in the iron foundry of Archibald Kenrick and Sons Ltd. John Arthur, son of Archibald jun. — a director of Lloyds Bank — became chairman of the firm. In 1878 he bought the *Free Press*, a run-down newspaper, to campaign for Liberalism, employing Frederick Thomas Jefferson as editor. From this grew the international printing firm Kenrick and Jefferson — the *Free Press* was disposed of in 1933. From 1920 to his death in 1933, John Arthur's son, Alderman John Archibald Kenrick, was chairman of Kenrick and Jefferson and joint managing director of Archibald Kenrick and Sons Ltd. He was elected to West Bromwich Council 1906, was Mayor 1911 and became a Freeman 1933.

KYOTTS LAKE ROAD Sparkbrook

Off Stratford Road between Henley Street and what is now Kyotts Lake Road. Beighton's *Map of Warwickshire*, 1722–24, showed a Foullake. A Kyott family purchased the land and re-named the lake, Kyotts Lake. Subsequently Kyotts Lake Road had a large tramcar depot. A Simcox family bought the Kyotts Lake property, and when they moved to Hall Green in 1874 they lived in Kyotts

Lake House. Just in Colebank Road from Stratford Road this changed its name to Cambrai House, and has since given place to Hall Green Technical College.

LADY BYRON LANE   Solihull

The wife of George Gordon, Lord Byron, the poet, lived here. Byron married Ann Milbanke Noel in 1815, but they parted after a year, she claiming Byron was insane. The Noel family had a large estate in Solihull and Widney Manor. Byron died in Greece in 1824, but Lady Byron, who died in 1860, regularly visited her Solihull home, and in 1842 founded an agricultural school at Copt Heath Farm. Lovelace Avenue (formerly Hytall Lane), off Widney Manor Road, is a reminder that William King, First Earl of Lovelace, married Ada Augusta, the daughter Lady Byron produced during her year with the poet.

LANDOR STREET   Vauxhall

Location of a British Rail Freightliner Depot. Walter Savage Landor was a poet born at the gracious Queen Anne Landor House at Eastgate, Warwick, now incorporated in Warwick High School for Girls. Landor once lived at nearby Bishop's Tachbrook, had a romantic association with Ipsley Mill, near Redditch, and is remembered, if at all, for an irreverent verse on the Hanoverian kings:

> George the First was always reckoned
> Vile — and viler George the Second:
> And what mortal ever heard
> Any good of George the Third?
> When the Fourth to earth descended,
> Heaven be praised, the Georges ended.

LANGLEY ROAD   Small Heath

Another Birmingham artist, Walter Langley, was rather younger than Henshaw (see under Henshaw Road). As a boy at the Midland Institute Langley excelled at clog-dancing and gymnastics on a railing in Paradise Street. Leaving a job as lithographer Langley moved to Newlyn, Cornwall, and painted so successfully that Count Leo Tolstoy called him 'one of the very few painters who understood the real function of art'. Painting mainly people, he died in 1922. His pictures in Birmingham Art Gallery include *Interior with Old Woman*, *Head of Greenwich Pensioner*, and *Men Must Work and Women Must Weep*.

LARCHES STREET   Sparkbrook

A road that enshrines much of Birmingham's history. 'Fair Hill', Dr Joseph Priestley's Sparkbrook home, was destroyed in the 1791 riots. Dr William Withering, eminent physician and botanist — discoverer of *digitalis* in the foxglove for the treatment of heart trouble — rebuilt the house and called it The Larches after two such trees he introduced there. Its position was at the

end of Larches Street farthest from Ladypool Road. For a while Thomas Attwood, one of Birmingham's first MPs (1832), lived at The Larches, his statue now standing in Larches Green. Around 1820 the banking Galtons occupied The Larches, and in 1822 Sir Francis Galton was born there — arguably Birmingham's most interesting son.

LAWLEY STREET

Vauxhall

Closely associated in older Brummies' minds with horse-drawn railway drays from the goods station, and still busy with traffic to and from the British Rail freightliner depot in Landor Street. Before 1832 Birmingham did not have its own MPs. It

Statue of Thomas Attwood, one of Birmingham's first MPs, in Larches Green.

was represented in the Warwickshire county constituency, which often led to conflict between rural and urban interests. From 1780 Sir Robert Lawley was elected as one of the two county MPs, a satisfactory acquisition by Birmingham freeholders who were almost unanimous in supporting him. It was said of Lawley by a leading manufacturer 'he hath been considered particularly the representative of Birmingham, and has often declared he was ready at an hour's notice to leave his home and go to London whenever he thought it could be of use to the trade of the town'.

LENCH STREET

City

With various Lench names at Harborne, Moseley and Balsall Heath. Lench's Trust, an honoured name in Birmingham, was founded on 11 March 1525, when William Lench gave his lands to his trustees to use the rents and profits 'for repairing ruinous ways and bridges in Birmingham, and to distribute the income to the poor within the town of Birmingham'. The income has mainly been used for building almshouses, and these still exist in Ladywood Middleway, Conybere Street and Ridgacre Road. Lench's Trust latest development is a block of fifty-nine units called Lench's Close off Wake Green Road, Moseley. The Trustees comprise four members nominated from the City Council and eight co-opted members, who choose a Bailiff.

LEWISHAM ROAD Smethwick

Birmingham district has several Dartmouth Roads, readily associated with the Earls of Dartmouth of Sandwell Hall until the mid-nineteenth century, then Patshull Hall. Viscount Lewisham of County Kent is the second title of the Dartmouth earls and the courtesy title of their eldest son and heir. Princess Diana's stepmother was Raine, Countess of Dartmouth, divorced from the 9th Earl, and married to Earl Spencer, Diana's father, in 1976. Colonel George Legge was created Baron Dartmouth in 1682 by Charles II and in 1687 appointed Admiral of the Fleet by James II to intercept William of Orange. He failed, and with William become king was sent to the Tower where he died in 1691. His son, William, was created 1st Earl of Dartmouth and Viscount Lewisham by Queen Anne in 1711. The 4th Earl (died 1853) developed West Bromwich collieries.

LIFFORD LANE Kings Norton

Spans the Stratford Canal at an exciting item of canal architecture, the guillotine lock which prevented the loss of water between the Stratford and Worcester canals. But why the Donegal name? Over 200 years back the hall nearby beside the River Rea was the home of James Hewitt who became Lord Chancellor of Ireland and took the title Viscount Lifford of Lifford in Donegal. So a town on the River Foyle near the Northern Ireland border shares its name with a house, reservoir, lane and district on Birmingham's Rea. John Dobbs,

One of the guillotine gates on the Stratford-upon-Avon Canal.

engineer to the Worcester Canal later lived at Lifford Hall which eventually became the canteen of a chemical works.

LIONEL STREET   Jewellery Quarter

Lionel was one of four children, all of whom died unmarried, of Charles Colmore and his wife Mary Gulston. Charles, who died in 1794, and is buried at Hendon, Middlesex, gave his name to Great Charles Street. Two of his daughters are remembered in Caroline Street and Mary Ann Street, near Lionel Street. While preparing this book I read in *True Ghost Stories of Our Own Time*, compiled by Vivienne Rae-Ellis (Faber and Faber), of a haunted chair at 16/17 Lionel Street. In an original building, then later in a new office block opened in 1959, the office chair used by a deceased Mr Russell was seen by three people with Mr Russell's 'ghost' seemingly sleeping in it!

LIVERY STREET   City

When Livery Street was opened in 1745 it was Birmingham's longest street, hence the saying 'A face as long as Livery Street'. The horsey name derives from Swann's Riding Academy which was on the corner of Cornwall Street in the later eighteenth century. The Albion Hotel on Edmund Street corner was the headquarters of Birmingham Old Contemptibles Association — survivors

of 'the contemptible little army' which went to the aid of Belgium in 1914. In 1953 Bruce Bairnsfather, the war artist and creator of "Old Bill" and his "Better 'Ole" gave the branch a fine war scene which acted as a sign, while the pub was called The Old Contemptible, as it remains today.

LOELESS ROAD   Lea Hall

The name is some distance from its origin in Yardley Wood. Here John Cottrell (Cottrell's Close, off School Road) founded a charity in 1715, now incorporated in the Yardley Great Trust Almshouse Charity. He gave property for the benefit of two poor widows — today the almshouses at 152 and 154 School Road, Yardley Wood, and 'directed that after the death of his wife Mary, a stone be affixed to a part of his house called LOELESS recording the gift of the house as aforesaid . . .'. Mary re-married, died in 1763, and the house Loeless was demolished around 1772. Loeless Road, with its neighbour Folliott Road, got its name from the Yardley Charities.

LOUISE LORNE ROAD   Moseley

An insignificant thoroughfare, mainly rear entrances between Alcester Road and Trafalgar Road, but it occasions some questioning. Louise Lorne was

John Cotterill's Charity plaque on almshouses in School Road, Yardley. (See Loeless Road)

Princess Louise, fourth daughter of Queen Victoria, who in 1871 married John Douglas Sutherland, the Marquis of Lorne, heir to the Duke of Argyll — so when he inherited the dukedom and Louise became the duchess her Lorne title tended to be forgotten. Princess Louise was an accomplished sculptor. The statue of Queen Victoria among the English monarchs on the west front of Lichfield Cathedral is the work of Louise. Her husband was the Ninth Duke. It was his ancestor, the Second Duke, who originated the saying 'God bless the Duke of Argyll' when his herdsmen also used the scratching posts set up by the duke for his cattle's benefit.

LOZELLS ROAD   Lozells

District and road get their name from Lowe's Farm which stood in the valley of Hockley Brook — once notorious for its flooding. Small hills rising from the valley became known as Lowe's Hills, easily corrupted to Lozells. In 1793 *Aris's Gazette* advertised the sale of Low Cells Farm of 138 acres. Aston Villa FC originated as Aston Villa Wesleyans from the Wesleyan Chapel at Lozells Hall. An early cinema, Aston Picture Palace, stood in Lozells Road. During the 1918 Spanish 'flu epidemic a Lozells Road barber, Cameron Robinson, went one Sunday and shaved six customers. By next Sunday all six were dead!

LUTTRELL ROAD   Sutton Coldfield

W Midgley in *Sutton Coldfield Town and Chase* accuses Sutton Corporation in the mid-eighteenth century of 'granting away its land to its friends', citing the grant in 1757 of 42 acres of Sutton Park to Simon Luttrell of Four Oaks who became the First Earl of Carhampton, though this was done by Act of Parliament seemingly with the consent of Suttonians. The beautiful Ann

Luttrell, widow of Christopher Horton of Catton Hall, Derbyshire, married, in 1771, Henry Frederick, Duke of Cumberland , fourth son of George II — who was so outraged that he caused the Royal Marriage Act to be passed forbidding royal union with commoners.

MACDONALD STREET   Balsall Heath

A Scottish family of Macdonalds came to Birmingham in 1820. Emily Street and Angelina Street, in the vicinity, are both named after members of that family.

MAGDALA STREET   Winson Green

Magdala in Abyssinia was the scene of a battle on Good Friday, 1868 in which Sir Robert Napier defeated the army of the mad Theodore, Emperor of Abyssinia, killing 700 and wounding 1,200 at a cost of only two killed and twenty wounded. Present were the young Henry Stanley (later of Livingstone fame) on his first overseas reporting job for the *New York Herald*.

MAITLAND ROAD   Alum Rock

Sir Arthur Steel-Maitland, Bart, was Conservative MP for Erdington (which included Alum Rock) from 1918 when Erdington constituency came into being, until unseated in 1929 by Jim Simmons (Labour). Erdington's subsequent MPs until 1951 were J F Earles, KC (Conservative) and Julius Silverman (Labour). By the 1955 election Erdington had disappeared as a parliamentary constituency. Sir Arthur, of Sauchie, Stirling, was Minister of Labour, 1924–29. He died in 1935.

MARGARET ROAD   Harborne

Named after Margaret Nettlefold who cut the first turf in 1908 of Moor Pool Estate, Harborne. This was the dream of John Sutton Nettlefold, one-time Chairman of Birmingham Housing Committee, a garden city of spacious sylvan fringes and narrow roads with nine houses to the acre. It was John Sutton Nettlefold who brought the Chamberlains to Birmingham. He was the uncle of Joseph, who came from Islington in 1854 to work in Nettlefold's screw factory as a condition of Joe's father lending Nettlefold a large sum of money to acquire a new American process for superseding hand manufacture of screws.

MARMION STREET   Tamworth

Robert de Marmion came with William the Conqueror from Normandy and was granted Tamworth Castle for fighting boldly at Hastings. He evicted nuns from a convent in the castle founded by Princess Editha. They moved to Polesworth Abbey, founded by St Edith (a different woman). When Marmion, also Lord of Polesworth, evicted the nuns again, St Edith appeared to him in a dream, struck him with her crozier, and he awoke with a wound in his side.

Suitably scared he allowed the nuns back to Polesworth. Editha is said to haunt Tamworth Castle and was reputedly photographed as a black lady in 1950.

MARTINEAU WAY   City

This road, and Martineau Square, off Bull Street, keep alive a great Birmingham name since the demise of Martineau Street thereabouts. Around the mid-nineteenth century Robert Martineau, a surgeon of Huguenot descent, came to Birmingham, and his family became part of the famous 'Chamberlain–Kenrick–Martineau' clique which did, and continues to do, so much for the city, particularly in education. Robert's son, Thomas (later Sir Thomas), became a lawyer, married Emily Kenrick, sister of Joseph Chamberlain's second wife, and was three times mayor. His son, Ernest, was Lord Mayor twice, and Ernest's son, Sir Wilfred, once 1940–41. Sir Wilfred's son Denis, recently Lord Mayor, is still a councillor.

MASSHOUSE CIRCUS   City

From Masshouse Lane beneath it, which got its name from the Roman Catholic Church of St Mary Magdalen built there in 1687/88 after James II's Declaration of Indulgence allowed Nonconformists, including Roman Catholics, liberty of worship. James himself gave 125 tons of timber from Needwood Forest towards the building, which had three altars and a convent attached. The church was consecrated on 4 September 1688, but within two months a Protestant mob had burned much of it, and within a few years not a trace remained.

MEDINA ROAD   Tyseley

Why, I had long wondered, was the second holiest Islam town perpetuated in Medina Road — though it perhaps becomes appropriate now that Yardley Grammar School, that was, is teeming with Moslem children. Considering Medina Road more critically for the *Evening Mail* series, I found one of the two roads off it is Havelock Road. So I looked up General Havelock, the hero of Lucknow (1857), but found he had never campaigned around Medina. Then, turning to Medina, Arabia, another entry reminded me of the little Medina River in the Isle of Wight. So, as another road off Medina Road is Boscombe Road — near enough to the Isle of Wight — I feel satisfied that Medina Road is Wight, not Arabia. Tamworth has a Medina among roads named after rivers.

MIDDLEMORE ROAD   Northfield

Isabel, heiress to Sir Richard de Edgbaston, married Thomas Middlemore in the fourteenth century, and their descendants held the Manor of Edgbaston for 300 years. In 1500 Richard Middlemore added a north aisle, and his wife Margaret the tower to what we know as Edgbaston Old Church. Their son, Humphrey, a Carthusian monk, was martyred in 1535 by Henry VIII — a window in the church shows him being led to execution. Sir John Middlemore,

Bart, founded the Middlemore Homes in 1872 — the first homeless children leaving as emigrants to Canada in 1873. Councillor Thomas Middlemore suggested 'Forward' as Birmingham's motto.

MIDLAND ROAD Sutton Coldfield

Alongside the Midland Railway, first proposed in 1871 as a line through Sutton Park from Whitacre to Walsall to connect the South Staffordshire coalfield with the Midland rail system. Alternative routes were suggested. Mercifully the chosen route, via Blackroot and Bracebridge, is more hidden than the rejected one over open heathland from Longmoor to Rowton Cottage. Hired gangs of Birmingham roughs broke up protest meetings in Sutton against both routes. In 1845 the London and North Western Railway had proposed a route from Birmingham to Lichfield, signing an agreement with Sutton to 'make a line avoiding the park, under penalty of £20,000'. The comma should have come after 'line', and when the scheme was abandoned Sutton Corporation, by legal chicanery, claimed the £20,000, but settled for £3,000 with which the old town hall in Mill Street was built.

MOILLIET STREET Winson Green

Jean Louis Moilliet came to Birmingham from Geneva aged 16. He married Amelia, daughter of James Keir, chemical manufacturer, and became naturalised as John Lewis Moilliet, a merchant. In 1815 he joined Birmingham and Warwickshire Bank which became known as Moilliet and Sons Bank, merging in 1865 with Lloyds when James Keir Moilliet, grandson of John Lewis, became a director of Lloyds Banking Company, retiring in 1877. The Moilliets bought Abberley Lodge, Great Witley, in 1836 and at great expense rebuilt it in Italian style — hence Abberley Street off Moilliet Street. The present head of the family, John Moilliet, still lives at Abberley, though not in the Lodge, now a school. The graves of several Moilliets can be seen at Claverdon.

MONTGOMERY STREET Sparkbrook

The banking Lloyds came to Birmingham from a house called Dolobran in Montgomeryshire — hence Montgomery Street and Dolobran Road near their home 'Farm'. They were a most prolific family. It was said 'The Lloyds are like weeds, they grow apace'. Keen emancipators of black slaves, they enslaved their wives with perpetual pregnancies. Charles (1748–1828) had fifteen children in eighteen years by his wife Mary Farmer to whom, in a letter, he referred as 'being in the old pickle' as though it were quite unrelated to him. Sampson Lloyd I (1664–1725) had sixteen children. Sampson II fathered four daughters in five years by his first wife before she died betimes. Sampson III and his wife Rachel had seventeen offspring, and when Rachel demurred Sampson replied 'Never mind, the twentieth will be the most welcome'.

MONUMENT ROAD   Edgbaston

So called from its proximity to Perrott's Folly in
Waterworks Road, off Monument Road. Built by
John Perrott around 1758, it was probably just a
purposeless eccentric folly, though it would have
offered a grandstand view of coursing on Ladywood Fields below. Its 139 steps raise the slim
tower to the height of 96 ft, and there are ridicu-
lous suggestions that Perrott built it to observe his
sweetheart's home in Five Ways, his wife's grave
in St Philip's Churchyard, and his ancestral home
at Belbroughton — through the bulk of the Clent
Hills? Declared an ancient monument in 1950 the
tower will always be associated with the names
of meteorologists Arthur Joseph Kelley and his
son Arthur Leslie Kelley who were directors between 1917 and 1967 of Edgbaston Observatory
— as which the folly was leased to the Midland
Institute in 1884.

Perrott's Folly.

MOORSOM STREET   Newtown

Captain Moorsom was one of the earliest members
of Birmingham Town Council. In 1836 a Bill was
introduced for constructing a railway between
Birmingham and Gloucester, and Moorsom was the
engineer in charge. Both Brunel and Stephenson
declared that the Lickey incline could not be
surmounted by a locomotive, and would have
diverted eastward — away from Stoke Prior's busy salt trade. Moorsom had
seen locomotives in America surmounting more severe gradients, so a number of
these were bought from Philadelphia. One of these was erroneously copied by the
stonemason on Bromsgrove's famous railwayman's gravestones in St John's
churchyard. It was a different tank engine 'Surprise' which exploded and killed
them.

MOOR STREET   City

Moor Street, long ago Molle Street, once housed the Public Offices, a gaol, and later
Moor Street Warehouse. Moor Street Station was opened in 1909, completed in
1914. Now a cul-de-sac, Moor Street once had a tram track. Tramcars from Digbeth
turned up Moor Street, left up Henns Walk, and left and left again to Dale End
and Albert Street termini. Henns Walk, now gone, had Birmingham's first graffito.
Beneath Henns Walk some wag had painted 'Cocks Run'. A building on the Dale

One of the railman's gravestones in St John's churchyard, Bromsgrove. (See Moorsom Street)

End corner bore an ancient lights notice. Dr Priestley's New Meeting House in Moor Street was burned down in the 1791 riots.

MOUNT PLEASANT

Bordesley

This little road off Kingston Hill was the drive to Bordesley Hall in its 30 acre deer park, the home of John Taylor, an original partner in Taylor and Lloyds Bank, now Lloyds Bank. The hall was devastated in the Priestley Riots (1791). Bordesley Park Road, obliterated by Small Heath Highway, was named because it cut through Bordesley Hall grounds. The Old Lodge pub, demolished 1986, on Bordesley Park corner, was a lodge of the hall — another was a shoe repairer's shop on Herbert Road corner.

MUNTZ STREET   Small Heath

George Frederick Muntz (Liberal) represented Birmingham in Parliament from 1840 until his death in 1857. He was responsible for the perforation of our postage stamps, and ensured that the man who perfected the process was amply rewarded. From 1868 until 1885, when Birmingham's representation of three MPs was replaced by seven separate constituencies, George's son, Philip Henry Muntz was a Liberal MP. He had been the town's second mayor in 1839–41. The Muntz family came from the Minsk Palatinate, Poland, and lived at Umberslade Hall, Hockley Heath. They founded the firm of Muntz Metals at French Walls, Smethwick — Muntz metal was an invention for making bolts, nails and ship's sheathing. The family still holds the Lordship of the Manor of Tanworth-in-Arden. Small Heath Alliance, forerunner of Birmingham City FC had their ground in Muntz Street.

MYNORS CRESCENT   Wythall

Well remembered are the sisters Emily Mary and Florence Anne Mynors of Weatheroak Hall, now Kings Norton Golf Club headquarters, who in 1908 built the spectacular belfry of Wythall Church in memory of their parents. The family originated in Uttoxeter, Staffordshire. Robert Mynors, who lived in Birmingham's famous Old Square around 1770, was a surgeon and male midwife. He was the author of a treatise on trepanning and an essay on amputation. He combined improved surgical methods with a considerable skill in operating.

NAVIGATION STREET City

Older Brummies remember the great queues for the 70 tram to the Lickey Hills each bank holiday. The term 'navvy' derives from the workers who dug the 'navigations' or canals, and Navigation Street was close to the canal offices and wharf off Suffolk Street when the Birmingham–Wolverhampton Canal opened in 1769. The water-borne coal from Black Country mines brought the price per cwt down to 4½d (*see also* Freeth Street). Spicer's taxidermist shop was on Navigation Street corner.

NEVADA WAY

Chelmsley Wood

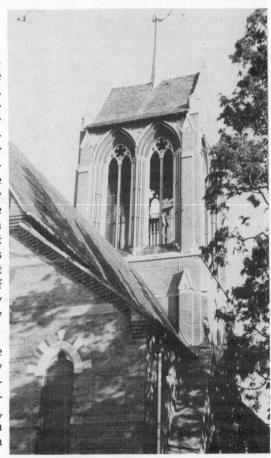

Nevada — so we study the street map for nearby Texas, Kentucky, Oregon ... unsuccessfully! Why, of fifty United States, pick on Nevada? Still searching for clues we find, next to Nevada Way, Wheatcroft Close — and was not Harry Wheatcroft a famous rose grower, and isn't Nevada a rose? So while we might not know why Wheatcroft is here we can assume that Nevada's here because of him. And with Piccadilly Close nearby we surely have another rose.

Tower block names are also fascinating. Chelmsley Wood has an academic collection in Oriel, Keble, Balliol, Somerville, Downing, Selwyn, etc. There's an archipelago of islands in Lundy, Orkney, Rathlin, Wight, etc. and while Severn, Tyne and Forth

The spectacular belfry on the tower of Wythall Church. (See Mynors Crescent)

initially suggest rivers, Menai, Tower and Waterloo confirm a bridges theme.

NEW BRIDGE   Small Heath

A medal was struck to commemorate the opening on 8 October 1904, by the Lord Mayor, Sir Hallewell Rogers, of this fine 200 yds structure across the railway and canal connecting Small Heath (Jenkins Street) with Sparkbrook (Kendal Road). One side of the medal has a representation of the bridge above the Birmingham coat-of-arms, the other Sir Hallewell himself. Such a bridge had first been suggested in 1880 — its eventual cost was £50,000 and it made a crossing half way between Small Heath Station and Sandy Lane.

NEWBRIDGE ROAD   Hay Mills

Off Hobmoor Road and thought by many to refer to the new bridge across the River Cole in Hobmoor Road near its junction with Newbridge Road. Mr A J Gardner of Birmingham 34 wrote to point out that the 1834 Ordnance Map names the 1825 hump-backed bridge across Yardley Green Lane (now Road) as 'New Bridge', and that a Newbridge Lane ran between Hob Moor and Yardley Green Lanes in the nineteenth century, obviously named after the Yardley Green bridge — which is the next downstream from the Hobmoor Road bridge. The Yardley Green bridge once had a stone block set in it with a vertical line marking the boundary of Warwickshire and Worcestershire, formed by the River Cole, and the date of construction 1825.

NEW ENGLAND   Bordesley

It's not in the A to Z, but the nameplate can clearly be seen from the bus in Bordesley High Street. Look along Adderley Street across the side of the large car showroom. New England can only have been a narrow passage. Adderley Street, with Bowyer Street nearby, suggests Charles Bowyer Adderley (the first

Lord Norton). He was Under-Secretary of the Colonies, 1866-68. Could it be that colonies then being populated were often known as New England?

NEWMAN WAY   Rubery

Cardinal John Henry Newman was buried at the Oratory Retreat, Leach Green Lane, close to Newman Way, in 1890. An Anglican clergyman, he was born in London, ordained 1824, became curate St Clement's, Oxford, and was active in the ritualistic Oxford Movement. Newman was received into the Roman Catholic Church in 1845, and founded the Oratory of St Philip Neri, Alcester

Street, Birmingham with four other priests and six lay brothers living on a weekly £4 offertory from Irish immigrants. He founded and financed Birmingham Oratory, Hagley Road, with a personal gift. He was created cardinal 1879; wrote the hymn *Lead Kindly Light*. His canonisation is being sought.

NEW MEETING STREET   City

Almost obliterated, but visible from Moor Street Queensway parallel with Carrs Lane, this street enshrines some Birmingham history. The New Meeting House was opened for worship in 1732 by Presbyterians in Moor Street, off which New Meeting Street ran. It was ministered by two pastors along with the Presbyterian Chapel at Coseley. During the 1791 Priestley Riots the New Meeting house was completely gutted by the rioters and its valuable theological library destroyed. For some years in the 1940s and 1950s Dan Davis's Everyman Café in New Meeting Street was a regular haunt of Birmingham socialists.

NEWPORT ROAD   Castle Bromwich

This is the Shropshire Newport. The courtesy title, Viscount Newport, is bestowed on the heirs to the Earls of Bradford, the Bridgemans, Bradford also being a Shropshire location. John Bridgeman in 1657 purchased the manors of Hodge Hill and Castle Bromwich. He, and subsequent Bridgemans, until earlier this century lived at Castle Bromwich Hall, often visited by Disraeli, an admirer of Selina, wife of the Third Earl of Bradford; and by Queen Mary, a great friend of Ida, the Fourth Earl's Countess. The present Bridgeman seat is Weston Park, Shropshire, near Newport; though the family church is at Tong, where the great bell is rung on the birth of a Viscount Newport or his heir, and tolled on their deaths.

NEW STREET   City

On Samuel Bradford's 1751 plan of Birmingham the upper (Victoria Square) end of New Street was called Swinford Street. It had five houses and nineteen inhabitants, while New Street, one of Birmingham's oldest streets, had 105 houses and 649 inhabitants. The same plan named the western end of Colmore Row as Bewdley Street : with fourteen houses and fifty-nine inhabitants it was to become the Haymarket and Ann Street before becoming Colmore Row. Samuel Bradford named Newhall Street as Newport Street, while the present-day Edmund Street bore three names — Harlow, Charles and Hill Street, in that sequence from Congreve to Livery Street.

OLDKNOW ROAD   Kings Heath

Named after Dr James Oldknow, the second vicar, in 1841, of Holy Trinity Church, Camp Hill. As Birmingham's first High Anglican ritualist he sparked off a stirring history in Bordesley Rural Deanery. His successor, the

Revd R W Enraght, was admonished in 1879 by the Bishop of Worcester for ritualism — elevation of the Host, Signs of the Cross, church processions, ceremonial robes. Enraght persisted, and in November 1880 was gaoled at Warwick as 'contumacious and in contempt'. In 1883 there were riots when a Low Churchman, the Revd A H Watts, was appointed successor to Enraght — eighty police and a 6,000 crowd at a Sunday service, fisticuffs at the Easter Vestry. The feud continued in other Bordesley churches in the 1920s between the notorious Low Bishop Barnes, and High Clergy at St Aidan's, St Agatha's, and St Gregory's on Olknow Road corner.

ORPHANAGE ROAD   Erdington

A generation has grown up since the demolition in 1964 of Sir Josiah Mason's Orphanage, but there's still a bust of the founder on the Orphanage Road–Chester Road island. A Kidderminster boy, Josiah came to Birmingham to manage his uncle's imitation jewellery business; took over Perry's pen works and perfected the slit pennib. The works employed 1,000 when he sold it in 1875. He went into partnership with Elkington's electro-plating firm. In 1869 he opened his orphanage, reaching a peak of 350 children in 1889. Knighted in 1872, Sir Josiah founded the Science College in Edmund Street which became part of Birmingham University. He died at Norwood House, Erdington, in 1881. His motto was 'Do Deeds of Love'. He is also remembered in Mason Road, Erdington.

Bust of Sir Josiah Mason on the Orphanage Road–Chester Road island.

OSLER STREET   Ladywood

Birmingham is indebted to Follett Osler, a considerable meteorologist, for the revered 'Big Brum', the Art Gallery clock, presented by him in 1885. During the 1840s he had established on the Philosophical Institution, Cannon Street, a clock which was then Birmingham's official timepiece, checked by churchwardens *en route* for church each Sunday, and their church clocks regulated accordingly. When the standardisation of railway timetables necessitated local time being replaced by Greenwich Mean Time, many difficulties arose. Not in Birmingham though, for before sunrise one Sunday Osler changed the Cannon Street clock to GMT, the church officials set their watches and their church clocks, and the parishioners had all day Sunday to adjust their domestic clocks and watches.

PARADISE STREET City

You might expect some imaginative association between Paradise Street and Eden Place just across Victoria Square beside the Council House. There is none. Paradise Street began as a rough track leaving Birmingham for Stourbridge alongside a field shown on the map as Paradise Close. The emerging road took the name of Paradise Row in 1785, but was Paradise Street by 1792. Eden Place was cut in 1867 and named in honour of Dr Thomas Eden of Pebworth, married to a Colmore.

PARGETER STREET Stourbridge

Philip Pargeter (1826–1906), son of Philip Pargeter of Kingswinford, managed Shut Lane Ironworks. Philip jun., was a member of Stourbridge Board of Guardians for forty years; Staffordshire County Council; Stourbridge UDC; Worcestershire County Council. He was a founder member of Worcestershire Historical Society 1893, a Magistrate, and he founded several freehold land societies at Kingswinford, Amblecote and Wordsley. He bought land and developed part of Walsall — where there is also a Pargeter Road. Philip became glassmaker with Hodgetts, Richardson and Pargeter, and later with Red House Glass Works. He retired 1882. With John Northwood, Philip made a perfect copy of the famous Portland Vase. Warley has a Pargeter Road.

PARK STREET City

Off Digbeth. It ran alongside the 'Little Park' on the Lords of Birmingham's manorial lands. Nothing park-like today beneath the railway viaduct, except the old St Bartholemew's burial ground. There was once a 'fleapit' cinema where now stands the Royal George Inn — note the correct Union Flag of the Royal George period; minus the St Patrick's cross. The Murphy Riot, 17 June 1867, centred on Park Street — High Church mob versus Birmingham's 'Ian Paisley', a Protestant Electoral Association rabble-rouser. Murphy subsequently sustained injuries from a mob at Whitehaven, Cumberland. These proved fatal, and he is buried in Key Hill Cemetery, Birmingham.

PATON GROVE Moseley

Off School Road. Cllr Thomas Paton didn't like the name originally suggested, so fellow committee members said 'Right, we'll call it Paton Grove'. Thomas Paton was a Glaswegian, a marine engineer who served on Merchant Navy convoys across the Atlantic in the First World War. He came to Birmingham in 1929 as an engineer at Cadbury's. He represented Deritend Ward for Labour 1946–61 when he retired aged 70. Pettit Road, Kings Norton was named in a similar way after another councillor who opposed the names offered by the developer.

PEBBLE MILL ROAD   Edgbaston

Now Midland BBC headquarters, Pebble Mill Road was Birmingham's first dual carriageway with a central tramway. During the war tramcars were parked on this to avoid night bombing of depots. The Pebble or King's Mill stood on Bourn Brook near its confluence with the River Rea — owned in 1597 by John Kynge, a fuller. The fulling of woollen cloth by water-driven mallets was introduced into England at Pebble Mill, which later added a blade mill and a corn mill, and in 1890 was occupied by a dairyman, Henry Harrison.

PEMBERTON STREET   Hockley

This recalls a great Birmingham family. Between 1677 and 1680 Thomas Pemberton, descended from gunsmiths, built a mansion on Colmore Row and Bennetts Hill corner. His son, John, property magnate and ironmaster, built sixteen houses in Old Square, the hub of Birmingham society and wealth. After the death of his first wife, John made promises to two women and his Quaker friends had to form a judgement on their claims. The family had a brass foundry in Livery Street, but sold it to the Great Western Railway in 1898 and moved to West Bromwich. Charles Reece Pemberton forsook the brass business for acting and writing, and in the nineteenth century Oliver Pemberton became Birmingham's most eminent surgeon, and was an expert witness at the trial of Palmer, the Rugeley poisoner.

PERSHORE ROAD   Selly Park

Obviously a geographical name, but many people comment on the terrace of fifty 'Alphabet Houses' between Kitchener Road and Dogpool Lane with decorative stone nameplates above their front doors. These range in twos, fours and sixes of the same initial letter, all place-names, from Ascot to Jarrow (*see also* Fashoda Road). They were built by Henry M (Mickey) Grant who came to Birmingham from Leicester in 1890 with 18 shillings, became a builder, and died at Nice in 1926 worth half-a-million. On Kings Norton and Northfield Urban District Council, his name appears on the 1905 foundation stone of Stirchley Library, and his family name at the Grant Arms, Cotteridge. Mickey was archaeologist, local historian, antiquarian. He built houses in Erdington, Bournville, Kings Norton and Stirchley — all blessed with place-names, many of them Irish. With illusions of grandeur Mickey called his residence in Middleton Hall Road, Kings Norton — Sandringham!

PETER'S FINGER   Bromsgrove

Off Worcester Street. Derives — though I don't know why in Bromsgrove — from St Peter's Finger, the apostle's forefinger pointed heavenward as it appears in occasional pub signs. I have seen it at Lytchett Minster, Dorset. The 'finger' is thought to be a rustic corruption of *vincula*. St Peter *ad vincula* is 'St Peter with chains', referring to his release from the chains in which Herod Agrippa bound him, and celebrated on 1 August.

PIDDOCK STREET   Smethwick

The charitable Piddock family were well known in Smethwick, Handsworth and Harborne. A William Piddock Foundation, 1782, provided help in schooling and apprenticeship for poor boys of St Martin's and St Philip's parishes. In 1576 Elizabeth Cowper, alias Piddock, gave £40 to purchase land, the rent to aid the Handsworth poor, while these proliferating Piddocks of Handsworth, Harborne, etc., made provision for 'poor people, being decrepit, aged, or impotent; of honest life and good conversation, and not given to idleness, drunkenness, and other vices'.

PINFOLD STREET   City

The site of the pound or 'pinfold' in which stray cattle, etc were impounded in more rural times. It is alongside the former General Post Office building. Hill Street, on the other side of the GPO, refers entirely to the gradient, not, as some suggest, to Sir Rowland Hill, founder in 1840 of the Penny Post. The street's name pre-dates both Sir Rowland and the GPO building (1891).

PITSFORD STREET   Hockley

Once a large sand-pit which supplied sand necessary to local brassworkers and others. This sand-pit, with an additional 12 acres, was bought by a private company and laid out as Warstone Lane Cemetery, consecrated in 1848. It was taken over by Birmingham City Council in 1951–52, as was the other nearby privately owned Birmingham General Cemetery — normally known as Key Hill — first used in 1836. Vyse Street, into which Pitsford Street runs, is named after a family related by marriage with the Colmores and Smallbrokes.

PLYMOUTH ROAD   Redditch

The Earls of Plymouth once lived at Hewell Grange, Tardebigge, near Redditch. Their seat is now Oakley Park, Bromfield, Ludlow, Salop — all of which are now road names around Plymouth Road, Redditch. Most interesting is Unicorn Hill, Redditch — two unicorns being the supporters of the Plymouth coat-of-arms. The family surname occurs as Archer Road, while parallel with it is Other Road (pronounced with a long O) deriving from the customary forename of heirs to the title. The Lickey 'Monument' is to Colonel Other Archer, 5th Earl of Plymouth, from officers of his Worcestershire Yeomanry Cavalry.

PRETORIA ROAD   Bordesley Green

Parallel streets off Bordesley Green suggest development around the turn of the century — all Boer War associations. Colonial Road — the colonizing it was all about; Pretoria — capital of the Boer republic Transvaal; Churchill — Winston himself, captured by Boers but escaped; and Botha, a leading Boer general who became first Prime Minister of the Union of South Africa after the wars, and subsequently leader of the loyal forces against German South-West Africa during the First World War. Can Whitacre Road be a marriage of two British Boer War generals, White and Gatacre?

PRIESTLEY ROAD   Sparkbrook

Probably the best-known event in Birmingham's history is the Priestley Riots,

1791, when a 'King and Church' mob rose against Dissenters and Jacobins celebrating the first anniversary of the Fall of the Bastille with a dinner at Dadley's Hotel on 14 July. Though not present, Dr Joseph Priestley, Minister of the Unitarian New Meeting Chapel, became the major target of the mob, which burned down his home 'Fair Hill' and laboratory alongside today's Priestley Road. Priestley experimented with electricity, discovered the properties of oxygen, and invented soda-water, activities which with his religious dissent made him a devil incarnate to High Tories. Other residences of prominent Birmingham men were also destroyed. In 1794 Priestley sailed with his family to America; settled at Northumberland, Pennsylvania, and died there in 1804.

PRINCIP STREET   Hockley

We were discussing British institutions named after Nelson Mandela — Balsall Heath has a Nelson Mandela School. "We've a Birmingham

Statue of Joseph Priestley street named after a murderer", said one. He in-
outside the Central Library. stanced Princip Street, off Newtown Row, named,
                                            he claimed to have read, after Gabriel Princip, the
Bosnian fanatic who, on 28 June 1914, assassinated Archduke Franz Ferdinand, heir to the Austrian throne, and his wife at Sarajevo, thus precipitating the First World War. Alas, nothing so dramatic. Princip — as Princep — Street is on a map in the 1818 *Wrightson's Triennial directory of Birmingham*, and the

Princips were landowners in NE Birmingham whose land was being developed around the late eighteenth century.

QUEEN ELEANOR'S DRIVE   Knowle

Off Jacobean Lane, it has an association with Charing Cross, London. Eleanor was the 'chere reine', the 'dear queen' of Edward I who gave the manor of Knowle to Westminster Abbey. Edward married Eleanor, daughter of Ferdinand III of Castille in 1254 and had thirty-six years with her until her death in 1290 at Harby, Nottinghamshire; and wherever her funeral cortège stopped *en route* for London, Edward had an Eleanor Cross built. Twelve in all, only three remain — at Geddington, Hardingstone and Waltham. Charing was the last stop, hence Charing or 'chere reine' Cross.

RAGLAN ROAD

Including roads in Edgbaston and Handsworth there are twelve Raglans in the Birmingham A to Z — a strange tribute to the elderly and uninspiring Commander-in-Chief in the Crimean War (1854–56). His greatest feat was giving fashion to the Raglan overcoat. Raglan lost an arm at Waterloo, and often referred to the Russian army in the Crimea as the French, then our allies. His charger, Shadrach, lies beneath a ponderous Latin epitaph in the drive of Madresfield Court, near Malvern.

RANN STREET   Ladywood

One of the many casualties during Birmingham's development, obliterated by Ladywood Middleway. Joseph Rann lived in Old Square from 1771 to 1774. The Ranns were old inhabitants of Birmingham, originally butchers and graziers. They had a holding in The Shambles and amassed considerable property. The family

The Eleanor Cross at Hardingstone, Northamptonshire.
Photo: Tony Noble

then entered the professions as clergymen, doctors and businessmen, though one of them developed clay-pits and established a pottery works in the Lancaster Street area which originated the name Potter Street, another victim of Aston University development.

RICKMAN DRIVE   Lee Bank

Formerly the lower end of Bell Barn Road. Named after Thomas Rickman, the architect of St Thomas's Church, Bath Row. Building commenced in 1824 and the church was consecrated in 1829: it was destroyed by German bombs. Rickman, thrice married, was a scholar, and architecture owes him the terms

Early English, Decorated and *Perpendicular.* Rickman was the architect of Erdington Parish Church and two Birmingham churches now demolished, St George's, Hockley, and the Bishop Ryder Memorial Church. He had an office in Birmingham with Henry Hutchinson. He designed, with Hutchinson, the Midland Bank, Waterloo Street, and the splendid church at Hampton Lucy.

ROBIN HOOD LANE   Hall Green

Alas, no association with the outlaw of Sherwood, nor, as legend has it, with Maid Marian's family. The lane, the hotel, and Birmingham's largest traffic island, get their name from the misreading of a W for an H! In 1798, Sheriff's Plan of the area shows Robin Wood stretching from the junction of Stratford and Highfield Roads down to Trittiford Pool — crossing the present Robin

Hood Lane *en route.* Just down Shirley Road, behind the present Robin Hood Motel buildings, Temple Avenue occupies the site of a summer house known as The Temple in the grounds of Robin Hood House before its licensed days.

ROEBUCK LANE   West Bromwich

John Roebuck of Kinneil, Scotland, was a business friend of Matthew Boulton to whom he introduced a young Glaswegian, James Watt, who improved on the Newcomen steam engine. Boulton, dissatisfied with the power of Hockley Brook for his works, contemplated adapting a steam engine to lift water from the tail race of the water wheel back into the mill pool. Roebuck was backing Watt financially and limited Boulton's manufacture of the steam engine. When Roebuck became insolvent in the 1770s Boulton was a creditor and Roebuck relinquished his interest in Watt's steam engine, allowing Boulton to become a partner in it.

ROSHVEN ROAD   Sparkbrook

I know what it is, but not why it's here! You can travel straight from Sparkhill to Cannon Hill via Durham, Taunton, Brighton and Cromer Roads — some geographer wanted to get North, West, South and East respectively on the map. But why Roshven, between Taunton and Clifton Roads? Could it have been some railway enthusiast? On 1 April 1901 the Mallaig extension of the West Highland Railway was opened. It had originally been intended to terminate the line at the village of Roshven on Loch Eil, said on the Admiralty charts to be the best harbour on the west coast of Scotland. But feudal landowners fought it off, and Mallaig became the terminus and port for the Hebridean steamers. Roshven Road was shaken when a bomb destroyed the adjacent Carlton Cinema, killing nineteen, on 29 October 1940.

RUPERT STREET   Nechells

Off Great Lister Street, it commemorates Prince Rupert of Bohemia's part in the Battle of Birmingham, 1643. He was the great Royalist cavalry leader — the Roundheads are represented hereabouts by Cromwell and Oliver Streets. Rupert was Charles I's nephew. He is particularly remembered for his cavalry charge at Edgehill, 23 October 1642, chasing the Roundhead cavalry beyond Kineton when he might have been better employed on the battlefield. He later fought against Cromwell's Commonwealth at sea; then for Charles II against the Dutch, and became a trusted elder statesman.

RYDER STREET   City

Off Corporation Street beneath James Watt Queensway, named after Bishop Ryder of Lichfield who was most concerned with the spiritual welfare of

James Watt's home as depicted in a series of murals in the James Watt Subway (beneath the James Watt Queensway).

Birmingham people. He induced several wealthy landowners to subscribe towards the building of a church in Gem Street for the people of Gosta Green. He died before its completion. It was consecrated in 1838 and dedicated to him as Bishop Ryder's Church. Both Gem Street and the church have now gone.

Ryder Street saw an early Corporation housing scheme of two-storey four-roomed cottages built in 1889–90. There is a city coat-of-arms plaque from one of the old cottages on the wall of Aston University's Vauxhall Dining Centre.

RYDER STREET West Bromwich

Birmingham coat of arms, originally on one of the city's first council houses in Ryder Street, now on Aston University's Vauxhall Dining Centre.

With Ryders Green Road, named after a West Bromwich family which first appeared in the 1380 Poll Tax where Nicholas Ryder, farmer, and Christiana, his wife, were assessed at two shillings. In the 1570s a Robert Ryder appears in deeds and documents. His son, Simon, succeeded him in 1579, living at West Bromwich either in Dunkirk Mill on the River Tame or Dunkirk Hall. The present Dunkirk Inn, Whitehall Road, has nothing to do with the 1940 retreat, but is on the site of Dunkirk Hall. Simon was farmer, miller, landowner, and much in demand for his legal knowledge as manorial court recorder at West Bromwich, Oldbury and Halesowen,

RYLAND STREET Ladywood

Off Broad Street. John Ryland of Easy Hill (forerunner of Easy Row) was a civic dignitary and wealthy businessman of the late eighteenth century, of whom historian William Hutton wrote 'he had done more public business than any other... not only without reward, but without a fault'. He married a wealthy heiress, Martha Ruston — Ruston Street is parallel with Ryland Street. Their home was destroyed in the Priestley Riots (1791), but John left a fortune to his son Samuel who had an only daughter Louisa Ann, born 1814, who would, Samuel hoped, marry Lord Brooke of Warwick Castle. But she loved Henry Smith, and though he eventually married Maria Phipson, Louisa remained faithful, and after a life as Birmingham's greatest benefactress, including the gifts of Cannon Hill and Small Heath Parks, dying in 1889 she left her fortune to Henry's son, conditional on his adopting her surname — so he became Charles Alston Smith-Ryland.

ST AGNES ROAD
Moseley

From St Agnes Church, named after Agnes, wife of Canon W H Colmore, Vicar of Moseley Parish Church, who initiated the idea of a church to serve Wake Green area. The foundation stone was laid on 3 October 1883, followed by luncheon at the Skating Rink, Trafalgar Road. Consecrated on 29 October 1884, various additions were made before the 'Great Tower Mystery'. The vicar received a letter in October 1928 from London signed 'Caradoc', promising £1,000 towards a tower if another £1,000 were given — of which only £200 was offered, by J G Hammond of St Agnes Road. In 1930 'Caradoc' offered £3,000 if this or a lower tender could complete the tower. This was eventually done, and the tower consecrated on 29 May 1932, when it was revealed that 'Caradoc' was J G Hammond himself.

ST BENEDICT'S ROAD
Small Heath

Named after the church. The Revd H Jacob was assigned part of St Oswald's parish, and provided most of the cost of St Benedict's Church himself. Building commenced in 1909, but the church was not dedicated until 1920. It is in Byzantine style. St Benedict's Junior School opened on 1 December 1913 with ninety-five children. The first headmaster, Mr J W Monkman, served from 1913 to 1940, while a teacher, Miss P Cleasby, spent forty-one years at 'St Ben', 1923 to 1964. Appropriately enough, Benedict — along with St Nicholas — is the patron saint of school-children and of coppersmiths.

ST DENIS ROAD
Northfield

St Denis is the patron saint of Paris where he was beheaded as a Christian martyr on a hill famous for other things than Christianity, Montmartre. Legend has it that Denis picked up his head and walked a mile to a spot he preferred for his burial, now the site of the church of St Denis. He is therefore shown in church art with his head tucked underneath his arm, as in Sutton Coldfield Parish Church, and at Welford-on-Avon. Why Northfield has a St Denis Road I don't know, but I can tell residents that they can invoke their saint — against headache!

ST JOHN'S ROAD
Sparkhill

St John's Church was built between 1888 and 1895. Thereabouts the name St John's Road was given to what was previously Sturge Street, while Baker Street, which intersects it, was previously Jenny's Lane. Alderman Joseph Sturge, whose statue stands at Five Ways, was an anti-slavery campaigner, a Quaker who founded the Friends Sunday Schools in Birmingham. St John's spire was added in 1905. In 1922 St John's was known as the 'Twice Nightly' Church when, under the Revd F Mellows, 6.30 pm Evensong was followed by a second service at 8.00 pm to accommodate a phenomenally large congregation.

ST KILDA'S ROAD

Washwood Heath

Most people know that St Kilda is a remote island group west of the Outer Hebrides. Fewer know the identity of St Kilda. Says the *Oxford Book of Saints*: 'Virtually unknown'. 'No record of a saint called Kilda' says Charles Maclean's *Story of St Kilda*. Kilda is probably a corruption of Childa — a spring on Hirta, the main island of the group — it was not unusual to name wells after saints. Alternatively, it could have derived from a map-making error transferring to the group the name of an island near the west coast of the Hebrides called Skilder.

Statue of John Sturge at Five Ways. (See St John's Road)

ST OSWALD'S ROAD

Small Heath

There are two authentic English saints named Oswald. St Oswald's Church, Small Heath, is dedicated to the one I think of as the Unfortunate Saint. He was Bishop of Worcester from 961 until becoming Archbishop of York in 972. He died in 992 on 29 February, Leap Year's Day, so he is unfortunate in having his proper festival only once in four years, though it is usually celebrated on 28 February. Oswald of Worcester is unfortunate too in that the other St Oswald was King of Northumbria and a martyr, killed in battle by Penda, pagan King of Mercia, so that this Oswald is always depicted as a great fighting man with a large wooden cross which he raised against the heathen at Heavenfeld, and a sword in the other hand. He appears thus in a window at

Hampton Lovett Church, near Droitwich, while Oswald of Worcester is shown much smaller washing the feet of pilgrims. St Oswald's Church was built in the 1890s while Birmingham was in the Diocese of Worcester.

ST PAUL'S ROAD   Balsall Heath

St Paul's in Moseley Road, Balsall Heath was the church where eleven o'clock never came. Now it never will. St Paul's was demolished some years ago but St Paul's Road remains as a memento. The old church clock with Roman numerals had two nines — IX — and no eleven — XI. Roads with saint names usually take them from a church already there, and churches are more likely to be demolished than roads. Sadly, in Birmingham city, St Jude's Passage off Hill Street is gone with St Jude's Church and St Jude's Schools. There is a St Jude's Close at Maypole, another at Sutton alongside a St Simon's Close — the two probably being brothers, their joint feast day 28 October.

SAMPSON ROAD   Sparkbrook

On New Year's Day 1661, Charles Lloyd II of Llwydiarth, Montgomeryshire, a descendant of the kings of Dyfed, married a daughter of a Pembrokeshire man, Sampson Lort — so Sparkbrook has a Sampson Road. Charles was a Quaker, for which he spent ten years in Welshpool Gaol. His wife, allowed to live with him, bore two sons: Charles III and, in 1664, Sampson I, who in 1698 moved to Birmingham. He set up an iron merchant's in Edgbaston Street, and with his son, Sampson II, established a slitting mill on the River Rea at Digbeth. On 3 June 1765 Lloyds Bank originated in Dale End, the partners Sampson Lloyd II, his son Sampson III, John Taylor and his son John, button manufacturers, each subscribing £1,500 capital. In 1742 Sampson II had bought Owen's Farm and built the Georgian mansion 'Farm' in Sparkbrook, and Sampson Road runs alongside. There were eventually a Sampson IV and Sampson V.

SERPENTINE ROAD   Aston

A reminder of the Serpentine Ground and Onion Fair which sprang from Henry III's 1250 Charter granting William de Bermingham the holding of an annual fair beginning on the last Thursday in September — when people bought sufficient onions to last the winter. Pat Collins Fair was the attraction for years up to the closure. Aston Villa Sport and Leisure Centre now occupies part of the Serpentine site. The name seems to derive from the London Serpentine — a winding lake — opened by Queen Caroline in 1820.

SHAKESPEARE STREET   Sparkhill

Being on Stratford Road Sparkhill pays tribute to the immortal William with Shakespeare, Avon and Bard Streets. It also has, on Stratford Road, Ariel, Jessica and Miranda Villas, and Shakespeare House — aptly? — on an 'adult' bookshop near the Antelope. Little Inglewood Road has four 'Places' with engraved names: Rosalind (*As You Like It*), Cordelia (*King Lear*), Cymbeline (*Cymbeline*) — but who is Violenta? She is a citizen of Florence with a non-speaking appearance in Act III, Scene V of *All's Well That Ends Well*. Across Stratford Road, the first house on the left in Newton Road is Lea House. Look carefully, and you will see that some anti-Dickensian has obliterated the initial B and final K from 'Bleak House'.

SHAW DRIVE   Yardley

The late Alderman Dennis Thomas, Chairman of the Public Works Committee told me that while it was not policy to name roads after members of the City Council, when the Committee turned down Harlea, Thornsett and Horton as names for this new drive they named it Shaw Drive after one of their colleagues Cllr Shaw, a representative of Yardley Ward. The Council avoids tongue-twisters, over-long and obscure street names, duplicates of existing names, and prefers English to foreign names.

SHORTERS AVENUE   Warstock

Off Warstock Lane, and so named following a request in September 1951 by the British Legion to commemorate Arthur Shorter MM, a conspicuous Legion worker in the district. Mr Shorter lost a leg and gained the Military Medal in the First World War. He became a stalwart of Yardley Wood and District Branch of the British Legion. As County Pensions Chairman he did much unostentatious work on behalf of less fortunate ex-Servicemen. In 1944 Birmingham Council of the Legion determined to establish a committee to safeguard the interests of the disabled returning from the Hitler War, and Arthur Shorter became chairman until his death in 1951.

SHOTTESWELL ROAD   Shirley

Off Stretton Road, itself off Tanworth Lane, and with several other Warwickshire village names, is Shotteswell Road. I wonder how the locals pronounce it. Shotteswell is a village east of the Banbury Road in a peninsula of Warwickshire almost surrounded by Oxfordshire, and the inhabitants know it only as 'Satchel' — just as the people of Happisburgh, Norfolk call it Hazebro'.

SIR HARRY'S ROAD   Edgbaston

Who was Sir Harry? The question raised by this prestigious road became even more urgent with the advent of the Sir Harry pub in Pershore Road near its junction with Sir Harry's Road. Sir Harry was Sir Henry Gough, a merchant in the India and China trade, who purchased in 1717, from Lord Fauconberg, the Lordship of Edgbaston. Sir Henry's second wife was Barbara Calthorpe, and their son, another Henry, became Lord Calthorpe, taking that surname on inheriting the estates of his maternal uncle, Sir Henry Calthorpe. Subsequent Lords Calthorpe have retained Gough in their surname. The Warwickshire cricket captain on the 1920s, the Hon. F S G Calthorpe, son of the eighth Lord Calthorpe, was Frederick Somerset Gough. The Goughs were Wolverhampton wool-staplers who came to Birmingham at Perry Hall, Perry Barr, in the seventeenth century.

SIR RICHARD'S DRIVE   Beeches Lane Estate

Sir Richard Hamilton Anstruther Gough-Calthorpe made generous donations in 1937 to the Church of St Faith and St Lawrence in Croftdown Road. Off Augustus Road, Malcolmson Close and Niall Close are, respectively, the maiden surname of Sir Richard's wife and the forename of their eldest son. The Edgbaston road, Elvetham Road, takes its name from Elvetham Hall, Hampshire, the territorial title of the family baronetcy.

SMALLBROOK QUEENSWAY   City

Formerly Smallbrook Street, with the Scala Cinema, now Scala House. Named after the Smallbroke family of Yardley who took their name from a 'small brook' there. Richard Smallbroke built Blakesley Hall, Yardley, in the sixteenth century — now one of Birmingham's museums. Another Richard Smallbroke, a Fellow of Magdalen College, Oxford, owned priory lands in central Birmingham late in the seventeenth century — the site which became Birmingham's prestigious residential Old Square. Smallbrook Queensway was the first section of the Inner Ring Road to be completed 1957–1960. Its modern stores found it hard to succeed as the original shops had done. A shift in shopping focus was taking place.

SNOW HILL   City

One of Birmingham's best-known names, but with no known origin. Matthew Boulton of Soho Works was born in Snow Hill in 1728. Snow Hill can claim two 'firsts'. In 1781 Richard Ketley, proprietor of the Golden Cross Inn below Bath Street founded there the first known building society in Britain. In 1741 the 'Town Machine', John Wyatt's original weigh-bridge, was installed outside Birmingham Workhouse in Snow Hill — obviating the need to lift carts and contents in chains for weighing on a steelyard. The cumbersome Birmingham Workhouse Penny, minted in 1812, is a collector's item.

SOMERLEYTON AVENUE   Kidderminster

Why, at Short Heath, Kidderminster, is there a Suffolk intruder among a group of Worcestershire village street names? Somerleyton, near Lowestoft, is ruled benevolently by the Crossley family, the Barons Somerleyton, from their hall in its parkland. Sir Francis Crossley, Bart., MP for Halifax, Yorkshire, from 1852 to 1872, married Martha Eliza, daughter of Henry Brinton, the Kidderminster carpet manufacturer, the Crossleys being in the same trade. Hence a complimentary Somerleyton Avenue in Kidderminster. Halifax reciprocated with a Brinton Terrace, sadly now demolished. A branch of Crossley Carpets came to Kidderminster and closed in 1990.

SOMERSET ROAD Edgbaston

Frederick, fourth Lord Calthorpe (*see* Carpenter Road) married Lady Charlotte Sophia Somerset, daughter of the 6th Duke of Beaufort. Somerset and Charlotte Roads are named after her; Beaufort Road after her father, and Duchess Road in honour of her mother. Frederick was the youngest of three brothers to hold the Calthorpe title — and in turn three sons of Frederick and Charlotte became the 5th, 6th and 7th Lords Calthorpe, the 6th giving his name to Augustus Road. The 7th baron, Somerset John, in 1845, was authorised by Royal Licence to discontinue for himself alone the surname and arms of Calthorpe, and to bear only the surname Gough.

SOMERVILLE ROAD Sutton Coldfield

Mr Somerville of Sutton Coldfield asked me for some information on Somerville Road, Small Heath, and Somerville Road, Sutton Coldfield. It brings me back to the ubiquitous Digbys (*see* Dora Road) whom I have met as far apart as Dry Stoke, Rutland, and County Kildare. A certain Revd Charles Digby, Canon of Windsor, married Mary, daughter of the Hon. Hugh Somerville around 1800 — hence Somerville and Hugh Roads in the Digby territory of Small Heath. Knowing nothing of Somerville Road, Sutton Coldfield, I obviously began at a street map and found a Digby Road running off it and a Kenelm Road nearby, evidence of some Sutton Digby association. Kenelm is the forename of Digby heirs — hence Kenelm Road, Small Heath.

SPRINGAVON CROFT Harborne

Off Lordswood Road — and Shakespearian! Greaves Estates once told me "At Shakespeare's quatercentenary we wanted to commemorate the bard with Shakespeare Croft, but this was disallowed from duplication. So we chose 'Spring' for his birthday, 23 April, and 'Avon' for his birthplace". He added "We'd a director living in Lordswood Road so we went one up on him in naming Earlswood Court off Handsworth Wood Road. Nijon Close, off Sandwell Road links a director's sons Nigel and John, and our Kew Gardens, near Bordesley Green East, is the initials K E W of one of our men".

SPRINGFIELD STREET Spring Hill

Off Cope Street, beside the Ladywood Middleway junction with Spring Hill, and named after the mansion, Springfield, of George Hollington Barker, an attorney. He was famed as a numismatist and an orchid fancier. In 1803 his collection of tokens sold by Leigh Sotheby was described as 'the most complete series of Town Pieces and Tradesmen's Tokens ever offered to the public'. In March 1836 he despatched one John Ross from Falmouth aboard the *Opossum* to collect orchids in Mexico and Honduras. Barker once lived at 7 Old Square;

a subsequent occupant, Edward Cope, wine merchant, giving his name to Cope Street.

STEELHOUSE LANE City

St Thomas's Priory — 'dissolved' by Henry VIII — stood where now the Friends Meeting House stands in Bull Street, and its domestic rabbit warren was in Prior's Conegree Lane (coney — rabbit, is also an element in Conybere Street, Highgate). Prior's Conegree became Steelhouse Lane in the eighteenth century when iron from Sweden was imported as raw material for refining in Kettle's Steel Houses, and Samuel Garbett was refining metals with sulphuric acid on the site of the General Hospital. Samuel Galton, born in Bristol in 1719, married into the Birmingham gun trade and lived in Steelhouse Lane at Galton House where the Gaumont Cinema was later built. Samuel Galton jun. often entertained the Lunar Society there, and it was his butler who gave the famous name to these scientists and literary men who met on nights of full moon to facilitate travel.

Lunar Society plaque forming part of the mural illustrating the history of Old Square in the Old Square Subway.

STEPHENSON PLACE City

Beside New Street Station, obviously relating to George Stephenson, the railway pioneer. Also there, outside the Queen's Hotel, was a hackney carriage stand. So Stephenson Place became regarded as the centre of Birmingham, and to regulate cab fares blue enamelled plaques on lamp posts throughout the city bore the mileage to Stephenson Place. Plaques will be remembered by older readers at Lincoln Street, Balsall Heath 1½ miles; Ladypool Road Schools 2m; Belgrave and Bristol Road junction 1m; St Barnabas School, Ryland Street, Ladywood 1m; Hagley Road–Monument Road 1½ m; and Coventry Road, Small Heath, near Muntz Street 2m.

STEVENS ROAD   Halesowen

The stranger among roads named after Worcestershire rivers, Severn, Avon and Teme, it was intended to be called Salwarpe Road, after Droitwich's river, but the late Cllr Cliff Willetts insisted on Stevens Road after a farming family, one of whose fields was Joey's Field where Tanhouse Lane Flats now stand. Joey Stevens father sang continually 'We plough the fields and scatter' as he scattered seed by hand. Around the turn of the century Joey himself transported coal from Beech Tree Colliery, his cart pulled by a horse named Merriman. Joey would fill the cart with children leaving school, and leaving Merriman to find his own way, would drop the reins and beat time as the children sang hymns.

STUD LANE   Stechford

Named after a stud there at which Mr Graham bred racehorses.

Now a word on investigating the origin of street names. In *The West Midlands Village Book* (1989), Hall Green Women's Institute entry suggests that 'Studland Road was so called because horses were bred on land near Hawe Green Lane, and the locals called it Stud Land'. Studland Road runs off Lulworth Road, a Dorset name, and nearby is yet a third, Durlston Grove. The problem is: did 'Stud Land' Road get its name first and thereby suggest the other two Dorset names, or were all three named simultaneously by a developer with Dorset connections?

SUMBURGH CROFT   Castle Vale

Sumburgh is Shetland's airport. Castle Vale Estate was built 1964–68 on Castle Bromwich aerodrome. Its roads named after civilian airports in Britain include: Turnhouse (Edinburgh); Dyce (Aberdeen); Renfrew (Glasgow); Stornaway (Lewis), etc; and RAF stations: Tangmere; Upavon; Biggin; Padgate, etc. Tower blocks names after aircraft include: Hampden; Trident; Comet; Lysander, etc. The greatest name goes to a pub, The Lancaster. A second pub is The Albatross after the bird on the RAF badge. Test flown from Castle Bromwich during the war were 11,555 Spitfires and many Lancasters made at the Nuffield shadow factory across Chester Road.

SUMMERFIELD ROAD
SUMMERFIELD CRESCENT

Rotton Park

Summerfield Park constitutes the grounds of Summerfield House, the home of the Chance family — as a red marble drinking fountain once explained. The Chances also gave West Park, Smethwick in 1869. Chance Brothers, now part of the Pilkington Group, dated from 1814. In 1832 it was the first company in England to make sheet glass, and in 1851 it supplied over one million square feet of glass for the Crystal Palace at the Great Exhibition. The only company for fifty years making optical glass, Chance's also constructed lighthouses, and after 1945 an employee toured the Far East arranging the renewal of lighthouses destroyed in the war against Japan.

SUMNER ROAD

Coleshill

Bird's Custard Powder was produced by Alfred Bird without eggs which his wife's stomach could not tolerate. Ty-phoo Tipps (a spelling error which took on) tea comes from a large-leafed plant, minus the stalk, broken very small, thus reducing the tannin which upset the digestion of Mary Sumner, sister of John Sumner sen. From 1820 William Sumner and his descendant John of Coleshill had been in the tea business, but Ty-Phoo was their breakthrough. The firm moved from Hutton House, High Street, to Castle Street, now a narrow passage off High Street, Birmingham.

SWANSHURST ROAD

Moseley

From a Swanshurst family and a Swanshurst Farm (demolished 1917). In 1221 nineteen neighbours of Thomas Swanshurst were in dispute with him for hedging land on which they had common rights. Swanshurst Common survived until 1847, including the area of Swanshurst Park today. Swanshurst Farm, according to the Yardley historian Victor Skipp, was the home of the Swanshursts until 1453, and from 1480 to 1854 of the Dolphins. Folklore — supported by some Victorian antiquarians — has it that an 11-acre earthwork at Swanshurst, ploughed up in the 1820, dates from the last campaign of King Alfred, and might even have been the headquarters of the king.

TEMPLE STREET

City

In *The Making of Birmingham* Dent refers in the late seventeenth century to 'a temporary wooden construction erected on the fields which covered the site of Temple Street served as a Temple of Thespis' (Thespis — a Greek dramatic poet, hence Thespian for an actor). Strolling players put on the comical scenes from Shakespeare, and occasional higher calibre entertainment was provided by visiting actors. Cherry orchards grew hereabouts, Greenwood's in upper New Street, and Walker's on the site of what became Cherry Street.

TENBURY ROAD   Kings Heath

Presumably named after Tenbury Wells, but has a nickname unconnected with
that Worcestershire town. It is known as 'Politicians Corner'. Among past and
present residents are the late Alderman Wallace Lawler, Liberal MP for
Ladywood; Hon. Alderman Victor Turton (Labour) ex-Lord Mayor, and his
daughter Cllr Mrs Pat Sever (Labour); Hon Alderman Hilda Barradell and her
husband Cllr Barnard Barradell; and ex-Lord Mayor Alderman Stanley Bleyer
(all three Conservative).

TENTERFIELDS   Halesowen

From tenter hooks, made by Halesowen nailers, originally used to stretch cloth,
but eventually to hang anything — hence 'to be on tenterhooks' is to be in a
state of suspense. I have seen herrings kippered on tenter hooks at Yarmouth
above smoking wood fires. Self-employed nailers of Halesowen were so
exploited by foggers and tommy-masters[1] that in 1860 they went on strike.
Sam Scott, general dealer and bookseller wrote a poem of 105 verses to help
the nailers. It is probably the worst poem ever written but is a fine catalogue
of nails including 'And so sure as I've published this book; Can't do without
tenter or tiling hooks'.

THREE SHIRES OAK ROAD   Smethwick

The Three Shires Oak, which marked the boundary of Staffordshire with
detached portions of Shropshire and Worcestershire, was felled in 1904 leaving
Three Shires Oak Road and Oak Cottage as its memorial. Wigorn Road,
running off Three Shires Oak Road to Adkins Lane, is a reminder of the
Worcestershire connection, Wigorn being the old name of the county. The
Adkins family once lived in Lightwoods House, built 1780–90 by the Grundys
and now the studio of Hardman's, stained glass artists. A red brick, right of
the porch, is faintly inscribed 'Jonathan Grundy. June 19, 1790.

TIDESWELL ROAD   Perry Beeches

A Derbyshire village in the Peak district. Perry Beeches Estate was built in the
early 1930s by Henry Boot of Sheffield who named the roads after Peak
locations — Edale, Curbar, Sterndale, Longstone, Rowdale, Monsal,
Holmesfield, and Haddon — it was from Haddon Hall that Dorothy Vernon
eloped with John Manners in the famous love story. Henry Boot also built the
Pheasey Estate : houses completed there before the 1939–45 War were occupied
by United States forces who had their headquarters in Pheasey Community
Hall.

---

(1) The agents of the masters of the nailers — who insisted on the nailers
    buying their necessities in 'tommy-shops' run by the agents — or even
    paying the nailers in kind rather than money.

TILTON ROAD — Small Heath

At one end of St Andrew's football ground, and it is doubtful if the notorious 'Tilton Gang' of 'supporters' know that it is named after a Digby family seat at Tilton-on-the-Hill, Leicestershire. Nearby, off Garrison Lane, tatty little Venetia Road is named after the reigning beauty of James I's Court, Venetia Stanley. Venetia's husband, Admiral Sir Kenelm Digby, was so proud of her complexion that he tried to preserve it with 'vipers wine', which killed her in 1633. Admiral Digby died, like Shakespeare, on his birthday, 11 June 1665, leaving his forename Kenelm to be passed down among Digby heirs, and thence to Kenelm Road, Small Heath. Next to it, Swanange Road tells of the Digbys' present day Dorset connections.

TIPPERARY WALK — Oldbury

With Judge Close adjacent, this is Oldbury's tribute to Jack Judge, who first sang "It's a long way to Tipperary" at Stalybridge Grand Theatre on 31 January 1912. The tune was composed by Henry Williams. He and Judge sang it before 1912 with 'Connemara' instead of 'Tipperary' at The Plough, near Kenilworth, now the Tipperary Inn. Judge substituted 'Tipperary' for 'Connemara' at Stalybridge, and won a bet for composing a 'new' song. Both men received royalties from the music publisher. Williams's headstone (died 1924) in Temple Balsall churchyard proclaims him 'Author of Tipperary' — 'composer' would be more correct. Judge died in 1938, a memorial seat in Oldbury describing him, incorrectly, as 'composer' of Tipperary. He probably wrote the words.

TORC AVENUE — Tamworth

Near the Coventry Canal at Glascote, this unusual name records the discovery in 1943 of a 2,000 year old Celtic gold necklace or *torc*. It lay in the wardrobe at the home of one of the three finders for twenty-five years until its importance was suspected. It is now in Birmingham Museum, and the finders have split the £7,500 treasure trove between them.

TURCHILL ROAD — Walmley

Turchill, Lord of Warwick and fifty-two manors, was one of the Saxons not at Hastings who was wise enough to co-operate with William the Conqueror — a Quisling some might say. On William's orders Turchill constructed a defensive ditch around Warwick and built the town gates, of which West Gate and East Gate remain. Turchill took the name of Arden and his line multiplied throughout the county, eventually producing Mary Arden, Shakespeare's mother. Falstaff Close, off Turchill Drive, recalls Falstaff in *Henry IV, Part 1* — "Fill me a bottle of sack; our soldiers shall march through; we'll to Sutton Colfil tonight".

TURTON ROAD   West Bromwich

In 1583 William Turton of West Bromwich purchased Greet and Oldbury Mills
on the River Tame, and the family owned them for 150 years. William's son,
William,married Anne Smallbroke, daughter of a Birmingham ironmonger.
Dying in 1621, he left property in West Bromwich, Tipton, Barr, Solihull, Kings
Norton and Banbury. His brother Thomas founded a Hateley Heath branch of
the family, while another brother, John, purchased Oak House. Various Turtons
were trustees of the Pudding Lane Dole and the Brick Kiln Dole. One Eleanor
Turton 'of the mill' left £2.10*s* annually, chargeable on profits of the mill, to the
poor of West Bromwich and Oldbury.

TYSELEY LANE   Tyseley

The district name, Tyseley, is one of those least interesting of place-names
derivations, meaning the land cleared by some obscure and uninteresting
Saxon, in this case one Tyssa. A family called Tyseley appeared on the Rent
Rolls by 1327. There was a Tyseley Farm with a moat which was south of the
present crossing of Ferndene Road by Sunningdale Road. There was also a
Tyseley Brook which joined the River Cole near the present Warwick Road
bridge.

UMBERSLADE ROAD   Stirchley

Umberslade Hall, Hockley Heath, was the seat of the Muntz family, and Muntz
Park, off Umberslade Road, indicates some associations of that area with the
city fathers, MPs, and industrialists of the Muntz family (*see* Muntz Street).
Umberslade Hall was built 1695–1700 for Andrew Archer, architect of St
Philips Cathedral, Birmingham. Thomas Archer's nephew, also Thomas,
raised to the peerage in 1747, celebrated by building Nuthurst Obelisk near
Umberslade Hall. Sir Simon Archer (1581–1662) invited Sir William Dugdale
to join him in a *History of Warwickshire* which Dugdale himself produced. The
Muntz family came to Umberslade Hall in the 1850s.

UNETT SQUARE   Hockley

John Wilkes Unett, born in Lichfield Cathedral Close, became a partner in
Barker and Unett, Birmingham solicitors, and a landowner. He lived in Old
Square, and there Colonel Thomas Unett was born in 1800. He fought in the
Crimea with the 19th Foot. In 1855 he tossed with Colonel Wyndham for the
honour of leading the regiment on the final assault of the Redan at the siege
of Sebastopol. Colonel Unett 'won' — and was mortally wounded in the action.
There is an obelisk to his memory in St. Philip's churchyard. John Wilkes Unett,
leaving Old Square, lived at 'The Woodlands', Smethwick, where another
Unett Street and Woodlands Street run from Grove Lane to Raglan Road —
named after the Commander-in-Chief in the Crimea.

UPPER MILL LANE   Digbeth

Birmingham's shortest street, a dozen paces from Digbeth to Moat Lane. The manorial mill of the Lords of Birmingham was around the site now occupied by Digbeth Coach Station. Moat Lane is a reminder of the moat surrounding the Manor house, fed by springs and overflowing into the River Rea. When Town Mill was leased to Joseph Farmer in 1728 he was allowed to direct this overflow into his millpond every three weeks to supplement the flow which came from the River Rea via a leet. Westley's 1731 map shows Lloyd's slitting and corn mill occupying the mill site.

VAUGHTON STREET   Highgate

In the early 1800s boats could be hired at Deritend to row upstream on the River Rea to 'the lovely sequesterd and elegant pleasure gardens of Apollo House in Moseley Street'. Today Apollo Row marks the spot. Rowing upstream through meadows, cherry orchards, and parkland with deer beside the 'lively-tripping Rea' one passed Vaughton's Hole, where the head race of the Town Mill left the river. The surplus from the millpool was released into the Rea via Vaughton's Hole every third week. In 1816 a 'delightful garden' was advertised for sale in the avenue from Deritend Brewery to Vaughton's Hole 'with no probability of it ever being disturbed for building'. Alas!

VICTORIA ROAD   Harborne

England is criss-crossed with Victoria Roads, almost always accompanied by an Albert Road, as in Harborne. Here Victoria Road merits mention. From 1865 to 1869 Elihu Burritt was United States Consul in Birmingham, and has left us his famous book *Walks in the Black Country and its Green Borderland*. He lived in Victoria Road, Harborne in a detached house which he called New Britain Villa after his Connecticut birthplace. Leaving Birmingham in 1870 he hoped his housename might survive. It has — Nos. 9 and 11 Victoria Road bear the nameplate New Britain Villa, with the addition at No. 11 of Burritt's House — the later home of another writer, Edward Chitham, author of *The Black Country* (1972).

VICTORIA SQUARE   City

So called only since 7 February 1901. Previously Council House Square it was re-named with Queen Victoria's permission after the unveiling there on 10 January of the Queen's statue, when the Lord Mayor, Alderman Samuel Edwards, rashly declared 'it shall be preserved in its present position for all time'. So far it has outlasted Joseph Priestley, John Skirrow Wright, Sir Robert Peel and Edward VII in the square, though it is not the original Sicilian marble statue, this having been re-cast in bronze and unveiled in January 1951. The original statue was given in 1887 by Sir Henry Barber of the Barber Institute fame in memory of his father.

VIGO ROAD   Brownhills

Half-way between Aldridge and Brownhills, Vigo is a name widely used there for a farm, a terrace, a close, and Vigo Fault down Walsall Wood Colliery. There is also a Vigo district near Bromsgrove. 'Up the Vigo' is a common expression around Brownhills Vigo Road. Vigo Street, London, and probably three other Vigo names spring from a victory in Vigo Bay, Northern Spain, of a British–Dutch fleet over a Spanish–French fleet on 12 October 1702. The victory set Britain sneezing, the booty consisting of several Spanish ships loaded with snuff.

VINCENT DRIVE   Edgbaston

The main road leading to the Queen Elizabeth Hospital — as well it may, for Sir Harry Vincent gave £150,000 towards the building of the hospital, and his son, Eric, was equally generous. Harry Vincent was born at Evesham in 1874 and became a clerk with the Worcestershire Preserve Company. Aged 21, he left, and with £30 capital founded a confectioners and sauce business. After his business outgrew several premises, in 1925 Harry bought 90 acres at Hunnington, near Halesowen, for £4,600 and built the model confectionery factory which produced Blue Bird toffees. Knighted in 1939 Sir Harry died in his Priory Road, Edgbaston home in 1952. Eric Vincent died in Augustus Road in 1963.

VYSE STREET   Hockley

In 1937-38 some correspondence between the Birmingham City Librarian, H G Cashmore, and Major-General Sir Richard Howard Vyse concerned 174 deeds and papers relating to Vyse property in Birmingham and elsewhere which went to the City Library on permanent loan. Among these was Colonel Vyse's 'Premises Book' which listed leases in the Smallbrook Street area granted in 1867 to Joseph Watson, grocer; George Goodrich JP, manufacturer; Samuel Beeny, draper; and James Kent, boot and shoe dealer. A sketch map showed a Tonk Street off Smallbrook Street, and a Vale Street off New Street where a lease to Edwin G Keay was endorsed 'Sold to London and North Western Railway, August 1878'.

With a lease in 1883 to H E Jordon, basket maker, we find Station Street under construction. In 1884 a lease was granted between Station Street and Hinckley Street to George and William Coldicutt, undertakers, who were bought out by the present day undertakers, N Wheatley and Sons, who moved from their previous Hill Street premises. On 9 August 1900 William Butler took a lease on the Station Street – John Bright Street corner to expend £6,000 on building the Alexandria Theatre. In 1915 Thomas R and Ernest R (later Sir Ernest) Canning, drysalters, were granted a lease on the corner of Great Hampton Row and Constitution Hill to demolish all existing buildings, and to rebuild to the sum of £4,500 the premises we know as W Canning and Co. Ltd.

The 'Premises Book' continues with records of leases up to 1929 in Northampton Street, Augusta Street and Vyse Street in the Jewellery Quarter.

WAKE GREEN ROAD
Moseley

From a green on which wakes or fairs were held. Wake Green House occupied the site between the present St Agnes Road and Billesley Lane. In 1791 it was the residence of Thomas Lakin Hawkes, who had been publicly described by one John Lane as 'disaffected to Government'. Though in February 1790 Lane had been forced to withdraw this 'gross calumny', Hawkes was one of the victims of the 'Church and King' mob during the Priestley Riots, July 1791. Dr Joseph Priestley took temporary refuge at Wake Green House after his home 'Fair Hill' was burned down. Hawkes estimated subsequent damage to Wake Green House at £304.3s.8d, but was awarded only £90.15s.8d compensation.

WATTON GREEN
Castle Vale

After the late Alderman Harry Watton, CBE who gave up his job in printing when it interfered with his services on Birmingham City Council. He was chairman of various committees and an uncompromising leader of the Labour Party on the Council. In 1970–71 he held the prestigious office of Bailiff of King Edward VI Schools Foundation. Near Watton Green, Bond Drive remembers Cllr Ernest Bond, Chairman of the House Building Committee, while Thomas Walk commemorates the late Alderman Dennis Thomas, also honoured by a plaque in Thomas Garden beneath Holloway Circus, recalling that he was Chairman of the Public Works Committee 1959–66.

WEAMAN STREET
City

Beside the Post and Mail building. The Weamans were wealthy Birmingham landowners. In the 1770s Miss Mary Weaman gave land and money towards building St Mary's Church (named after her, but now demolished), its parish comprising an area between Lancaster Street, Snow Hill, Steelhouse Lane and the Birmingham Canal. The family benefited from a famous disputed will of William Jennens, reputedly the richest commoner in England — and a bachelor — who died aged 97. His £1 million would go to the descendants of one John Jennens, William's great- or great-great-grandfather. John married twice, his second wife, Joyce Weaman bearing him six children, to his first wife's five. John;s will was prepared by his father-in-law William Weaman with intent to settle the fortune on Joyce's children. Eventually, of at least seventeen litigants in a famous case, Joyce's line proved successful.

WEBSTER WAY
Walmley

Named after the Webster family of ironmasters of Penns Hall, partners in Webster and Horsfall, the Hay Mills, Birmingham, firm which in 1858–66 made the Atlantic cables. Five generations of Websters were in the firm beginning with John, born in 1687 at Normanton, who was married in Birmingham. His son Joseph I acquired the lease of Penns Mill in 1752 and drew wire there. In 1759 he took a lease of Penns House — now the hotel. It remained the home of Joseph II, killed in 1788 while hunting in Chelmsley Wood; Joseph III, died 1856; and Baron Dickenson Webster, a younger son of Joseph III, who died in 1860. The elder son, Joseph IV, became Rector of Hindlip, Worcestershire and, like his grandfather, died in 1858 after a riding accident.

WESTLEY ROAD — Acocks Green

Previously Well Lane, later Florence Road. Several Acocks Green roads once had different names from today. Arden Road was Quality Lane; Hazelwood Road — Dog Lane; Lincoln Road — Shawley Lane and Rowe Leasowes Lane; and Dolphin Lane, renamed after a local family was originally Green Lane. Gospel Lane, once Longley Lane, derives from a 'preaching' or Gospel Oak. Acocks Green comes from an Acock family mentioned in 1420. Richard and Matilda Acock were living at Gilbertstone House in 1495. In 1626 William Acock received from his father as a marriage settlement 'Acocks Green House and other estates'.

WHEELEY'S LANE — Five Ways

Derived from John Wheeley's Farm — attacked and damaged in the 'Potato Riots' of 1810. In 1672 the house of a William Wheeley was used for preaching. Wheeleys lived in Edgbaston Street, having a grinding mill in Edgbaston. They were of considerable standing in Birmingham: in the late eighteenth century they were coachmakers and lived in the prestigious Old Square, with coachmaking premises in Lichfield Street and Ashted Row. An entry for Francis Wheeley, coachmaker, of both streets, appeared in Wrightson's 1818 Directory.

WHISPERING STREET — Bewdley

A lover's lane perhaps? — 'For talking age and whispering lovers made' (Goldsmith). 'No' said a Bewdley woman. 'Smugglers from the river used underground passages and could be heard whispering by residents above'. Nonsense! An electricity sub-station in the street occupies the site of Bewdley's old plague-pit, and adjacent is the old graveyard of now defunct Christ Church, its headstones removed and converted into a pleasant garden of rest in 1949. Passers-by whispered in the presence of so much death. But why change so interesting a name to Westbourne Street ?

WILLETTS ROAD — Halesowen

The late Cllr Cliff Willetts was born at Two Gates, Cradley, in 1896 and attended Bethesda Unitarian School. Most of his working life was as a chainmaker — he retired from Somers after seven years there. He became superintendent of Two Gates Ragged School in 1924 and was a Methodist Lay Preacher for forty years, licensed to conduct weddings and baptisms. He was on Halesowen

UDC and Borough Council from 1935; was Mayor 1950–51; Alderman 1956–62; Freeman 1963; member Worcestershire County Council 1955–74; and in 1974 was elected to Dudley Metropolitan Borough Council.

WINDMILL STREET City

Off the Horse Fair, Windmill Street ran uphill to the elevated site of a windmill which dominated the Guinea Gardens where, for an annual rent of one guinea, a working man was able to enjoy his allotments — such 'gardens' occurred elsewhere on the fringes of Birmingham early last century. As development gradually moved uphill from the Horse Fair, engulfing allotments and woodlands, the Colmores gave a plot of land for a church to accommodate the growing population, and St Thomas's Church was built in Bath Row.

WITNEY DRIVE Tile Cross

An Oxfordshire enclave near Tile Cross Road has Banbury Croft (cakes); Charlbury Avenue (glove-making); and Witney Drive. Witney is the original 'quaint little old-fashioned town' of Ada Leonora Harris's famous song. The 'Old-fashioned House', in West End, Witney, was the home of her grandparents Charles and Maria Harris — the 'dear little old-fashioned pair'. The 'old-fashioned street' no longer has cobble stones to 'harass the feet'. Ada Harris's words were published as a poem in the *Grand Magazine*. Singer Ivor Foster read it and asked composer William Henry Squire for a tune, which Foster sang at an Albert Hall Ballad Concert on 14 February 1914.

WORDSWORTH ROAD Small Heath

Wordsworth, Byron, Tennyson and Waverley (Sir Walter Scott) Roads, named after poets? Not Wordsworth. On the Aston Tithe map of 1845 a Revd Christopher Wordsworth was shown as the owner of three closes of pasture in a triangle formed today by Coventry, Golden Hillock and Wordsworth Roads. It seems likely that the road being developed around 1876, the year when Louisa Ryland gave forty-three acres for Small Heath Park, was named Wordsworth Road after the clergyman, and preceded the other poetical names. Developed some years later, they kept up the poetical sequence of Wordsworth Road. Older Small Heatheans will remember H G Lansdowne's dance academy and gymnasium on the site now occupied by the Garryowen Club.

WROTTESLEY STREET City

Wrottesley Park, Wolverhampton, is the seat of the Barons Wrottesley. Wrottesley Street, beneath Smallbrook Queensway in Birmingham, gets its name from Henrietta Wrottesley, youngest daughter of Sir John Wrottesley, Bart (1683–1726), marrying Theodore William Inge of Thorpe Constantine, Staffordshire. The Inges were wealthy Birmingham landowners — hence Inge and Thorp Streets off Hurst Street, near Wrottesley Street. William Murphy, Birmingham's 'Ian Paisley' Protestant rabble-rouser, remembered for the

Murphy Riots in Park Street on 17 June 1867, was pastor of Wrottesley Street Church until the assault at Whitehaven in 1871 which caused his death in 1872.

WRIGHT ROAD   Washwood Heath

Named after Joseph Wright who, with his two sons, founded in 1845 the Metropolitan-Cammell Carriage and Wagon Company, Saltley. A coach-builder and owner of stage coaches, he realised that the railway was superseding road travel. Wright soon employed 900, producing rolling stock for almost the entire world, including many prestigious royal coaches for trains. Joseph died in 1859. Though a Nonconformist, with a fine impartiality Wright contributed £500 towards the building of the C of E St Saviour's Church at Saltley.

YEW TREE LANE   Yardley

Normally a thoroughfare came before a pub which then took its name — Maypole Lane before the Maypole; Robin Hood Lane before the Robin Hood;

Yew Tree Lane before the Yew Tree, which was not opened until 1925 having been built in the grounds of Yardley House which originally belonged to the Minshull family. Later it housed three generations of the Flavells, a family associated

Today, the only maypole at 'The Maypole' is on this pub sign.

with Yardley as the Flawells or Flavells, the latter name appearing in documents of 1465 — hence Flavells Road. In 1919 the Flavells sold Yardley House to Mitchells and Butlers who, for ten years before its demolition in 1930, leased it to the Bosworths, another well-known local family.

Index of Streets (excluding main entries)

General Index

An ideal walking companion

Let's Walk
by Mark Linley

Written for those who wish to join the increasing numbers who regularly escape the stresses and strains of modern life by walking in the countryside, in the hills and on the mountains, *Let's Walk*, in its sixteen chapters, gives advice and information on clothing and equipment, where to go, walking holidays, map and compass reading, wildlife, difficulties and hazards, first aid, weather, and much else.

The author, as well as being an experienced rambler, is also a skilled artist and the book is lavishly illustrated with cartoons which give a lively view of the walking scene.

"A splendid introduction to rambling. Give it to your children, in-laws, colleagues, neighbours. Or enjoy the wealth of information and 100 cartoons/sketches yourself." *The Rambler*

ISBN 1 869922 03 4. 144 pages. £4.95

Meridian Books
40 Hadzor Road, Oldbury, Warley, West Midlands B68 9LA